BRAQUE

SERGE FAUCHEREAU

BRAQUE

RIZZOLI
NEW YORK

©*1987 Ediciones Polígrafa, S. A.*

Translation by Kenneth Lyons
Reproduction rights A.D.A.G.P., Paris - L.A.R.A., S.A., Madrid

First published in the United States
of America in 1987 by:

𝓡*IZZOLI INTERNATIONAL PUBLICATIONS, INC.*
597 Fifth Avenue/New York 10017

Library of Congress Cataloging-in-Publication Data

Faucherau, Serge.
  Braque.

  Bibliography: p.
  1. Braque, Georges, 1882-1963. 2. Artists—France—
Biography. I. Title.
N6853.B7F38   1987   709'.2'4   87-45392
ISBN 0-8478-0794-0

Printed in Spain by La Polígrafa, S. A.
Parets del Vallès (Barcelona)
Dep. Leg.: B. 24.546 - 1987

CONTENTS

BRAQUE WITHOUT A LEGEND

In all his life, Georges Braque never appeared in the gossip columns or created the slightest uproar in society at large—in sharp contradistinction to his great friend Pablo Picasso or to all those other painters whose highly colored legends have gained them so much popularity: painters such as Van Gogh, Gauguin, Modigliani.... If Braque sometimes scandalized people at the beginning of his career, it was because the radical novelty of his work was so utterly disconcerting; any such scandal would certainly not have been welcomed by such a deeply reserved man as Braque. As for his work, it has never enjoyed the favor of a large public as has that of several of his contemporaries. It rarely possesses the dazzling colors or the elegant drawing of Matisse; nor the virtuosity and inspiration of Picasso, let alone the latter's touches of sentimentality (pathetic characters, simpering children) or his no less conspicuous eroticism; nor even the robust, attractive imagery of Léger.... In Braque there is neither symbolism nor message, biblical or any other kind. His birds are birds, not doves of peace, and his characters are not naked because they are supposed to represent "the golden age," "the joy of living," dryads, or martyrs, but because they have quite simply taken their clothes off. The poet Blaise Cendrars perceived this very clearly when, at a very early stage in the artist's career, he described Braque as "a pure spirit" and "a Jansenist."

Another poet, Pierre Reverdy, a lifelong friend of Braque, recommends: "If one wishes to reach the art, one must sometimes begin with the man" (*Self Defense*). Since Braque, although he failed to fascinate the crowds, attracted considerable attention from writers and poets, it is the opinion of the latter that we would do best to follow. But in order to "begin with the man" is it really necessary for us to go through the social chronicles of the period—to report, for instance, André Salmon's account of the banquet held in Picasso's studio in honor of the Douanier Rousseau, or to recall the time when Braque piloted an old divan on casters down the slopes of the Butte de Montmartre, pursued by the shouts of passersby? However amusing they may be, such anecdotes do not take us very far in our investigation of Braque's work. Must we then follow the apparent formalism of Francis Ponge and—remarking how the painter's surname recalls such words as *barque* (boat), Bach, or Baroque—use this as our starting-point in approaching some of the themes of his *œuvre?* What Ponge does, he does well; as a result of his theories, however, we have heard—even in places with a reputation for earnestness, such as the Centre Georges Pompidou in Paris—more than one lecturer asserting, in an attempt at emulation and on the authority of some rudimentary notions of psychoanalysis, that Braque painted birds because his surname meant "gun dog" (*brach*, a retriever).... We know that Reverdy did not appreciate this sort of wit any more than he did the interpretation of anecdotes, and Braque was probably of much the same mind. Beginning with the man in order to reach his art means simply that we must not forget that at the origin of the work there is always a man working, investigating, advancing. In this book, then, I shall endeavor to follow Braque's work in its relation to his personal development. Since a good number of eminent writers have concerned themselves with that work, I will be relying on them as often as possible; their opinions, together with those expressed by the painter himself, will most reliably support such personal points of view as may be advanced in addition.

FROM LE HAVRE TO FAUVISM

Athough he was born in Argenteuil-sur-Seine in 1882, Georges Braque spent practically all of his childhood in Le Havre, where his father ran a painting and decorating business and was a keen amateur painter of landscapes in his spare time. The artist's grandfather had also been a painter and decorator; as may be seen, therefore, Braque was familiar with paints and paintbrushes from a very early age. Since he showed little interest in his secondary studies, he was apprenticed to a painter and decorator, but at the same time he attended evening classes at the municipal Fine Arts School of Le Havre (1897). It was there that he met two other painters who became great friends of his and, being a little older, were to encourage and influence him for several years: Raoul Dufy and Othon Friesz.

In 1899 Braque left for Paris, where Friesz was already staying; and the trio of young artists from Le Havre was to be reunited when Braque and Friesz were joined by Dufy in 1900. Unlike his two friends, however, Braque had not come to Paris to be an artist but first of all, and most particularly, to complete his training as a house painter and decorator, although this did not prevent him from attending evening classes in painting at the same time—a sign of the artist's modesty and prudence in the face of any new developments in his career. Only a few works have survived from this period: some landscapes in a rather heavy style and portraits of friends and relatives somewhat hesitantly painted, in which the influence of Corot tempers the softer lyricism of Impressionism. It was not until 1902, after he had completed his apprenticeship as a painter and decorator and had finished his military service, that Braque decided, with the consent and assistance of his family, to give himself up entirely to the fine arts. But of his crucial years as a craftsman nothing was ever forgotten, as we shall see. He rented a studio in Montmartre and embarked on a course of serious study, frequenting the galleries and attending academic courses, although he gave up the latter in 1904. The works still extant from this period (1902-05) are mostly seascapes; and the Pointillist style—or, more exactly, some features of that style—in some of them show that he was then interested in the work of Seurat, Cross, and Signac, and that the canvases he was to paint around Antwerp in 1906 did not represent such a radical break as some critics like to believe. But such works are now rare, for many have been lost, and others were destroyed by the painter himself a few years later, when he had come to see them as merely immature exercises.

Unlike his friends Dufy and Friesz, who were exhibiting constantly (as was Picasso, whom he did not yet know), Braque took his time. He did not exhibit his first canvases until 1906, when he showed at the Salon des Indépendants. Nor is it certain that he was satisfied with the works he showed there, which were not yet Fauve. At the previous year's Salon d'automne he had seen the room devoted to the Fauves, which had stupefied the public; and many years later he was to admit that it was the works of Matisse and Derain that had determined his "conversion" to Fauvism. He had also seen, at the 1905 Salon des Indépendants, a retrospective exhibition of Van Gogh, whose works, movement and pure colors must have impressed him greatly. Most probably the works of Dufy and Friesz, who were already Fauvist, had nothing to do with this so-called conversion, which was really a very rapid evolution rather than a sudden change of direction. For his admirers, and for Braque himself, his *œuvre* properly speaking begins with the Fauve pictures that he painted in and around Antwerp when he spent the summer of 1906 there in the company of Friesz.

Here I must insert a parenthesis. Who can possibly believe that a serious painter could change his style overnight? And yet, if we are to go by these alleged "influences," it was thus that it came about: Braque saw some Fauve canvases and at once became a Fauvist in his turn. And later we are presented with the same explanation: Braque saw *Les demoiselles d'Avignon* and at once renounced his Fauvist faith. But such a linking of cause and effect is far too facile to permit the slightest consideration of the process of artistic creation. Even when the evidence is first-hand it is all the more questionable, inasmuch as it has been given long after the event; writers of memoirs can be capricious, depending on their sympathies or on what they are trying to prove. I prefer, therefore, to mistrust such interpretations as may be taken from them and to confine myself to the works themselves.

In the 1950s, almost half a century later, Braque gave an interesting explanation: "The painting of the Fauves had impressed me because of what was new in it, and that was what I needed.... It was a very enthusiastic sort of painting, which was just right for me at the age of twenty-three.... Since I did not like Romanticism, this physical painting pleased me." (Interview with Dora Vallier, 1954). For lack of works of the period, and as there is little documentary evidence regarding Braque's transition to Fauvism, people have been rather too quick to conclude from the above statement that, just because he was "impressed" and "enthusiastic," he plunged all of a sudden into a totally new style. Does he not say, however, that he did not like "Romanticism"? That hardly tallies with a mere whim—anything for novelty—on the young man's part. In his earliest works Braque had never shown any penchant for either meticulous realism or the convolutions and mysteries of symbolism; he had passed over the lyrical effusions of the Impressionists for the more carefully considered researches of the Neo-Impressionists. In Fauvism he was to appreciate the gesture, the "physical" aspect of that painting. But was there not already something of that in those few earlier works of his that have come down to us? These display already a simplification of the drawing in which the color and the forms were reduced to elongated lines, mere strokes of the brush.

As for the brilliant colors characterizing most of the Fauvists' paintings, Braque only came to these by stages. Among the pictures he painted at Antwerp there are two almost exactly similar versions of *The Port of Antwerp*. In one, which is in the Kunstmuseum in Basel, three large ships are decked out in all their flags, and in the other (Von der Heydt Museum, Wuppertal), seen from only a slightly different angle, the ships are different and devoid of flags. The first version is characterized by a greater attention to detail and, therefore, a more sustained realism (the windows in the houses, the interior of the covered landing stage, the funnels and rigging of the ships, reflections on the water and the shapes of clouds); all of this is conveyed by the use of little touches of color that are certainly not very realistic (the church tower is violet), but are in general muted, rarely pure. The second work, which is as different from the other as a Derain of that period is from a Marquet, is freer as regards motif and might very well have been painted not in the open air but in Braque's studio, using the first version as a model. The patches of color are clearer and more strongly contrasted, vigorously brushed for the sky and the water, or in long strokes of pure yellow for the quay and the canvas tilt. Everything is more schematic and yet cleaner, for the colors sound a higher, truer note, without the least concern for veracity: the tug is a black shape in the pink and emerald of the water, the formerly violet church tower is given an intense green that stands out clearly against the tender pink of the sky. The one drawback is that the perspective is rather impaired by the presence in the background of a long and disproportionately large ship, larger than the buildings and the ship in the foreground.

In the autumn of 1906 Braque left Paris for L'Estaque, a little port near Marseilles. Attracted by the blue skies and brilliant air of the region, where the sun divides light and shade so much more sharply than in the Île-de-France, he was to remain there for several months. The canvases he painted at L'Estaque are richer and more complex than those he had done in Antwerp. A certain *Landscape near L'Estaque* (Musée National d'Art Moderne, Paris) reveals that Braque had studied not only the works of the Fauves but also the lessons of their precursors. Massive shapes with blue shadows, the rocks and the trees confined by rings, are reminiscent of Gauguin, a retrospective show of whose work had in fact been presented at the Salon d'automne that year. The characters walking up the lane, on the other hand, seem to have come straight from a canvas by Van Gogh, and the treatment of the earth in the foreground, with its broad, almost rectangular strokes of pure color, goes beyond the Neo-Impressionism of Signac and brings us to Fauvism, that of Matisse in *Luxe, calme et volupté* (1904-05), or that of Derain in 1905 or 1906, particularly in the works painted in London. But while in those painters the patch of color tends towards a point, in Braque's work it is stretched out to form a sort of little rod, or even a ribbon. This was a technique that he was to use fairly often, particularly when he wanted to suggest the iridescence of water—as, for instance, in *The Port of L'Estaque*. In the brilliant light of the Midi the pinks and soft greens of the canvases painted at Antwerp give way to vivid reds and intense greens and

The Ship Decked with Flags at Antwerp. 1906. Oil on canvas, 50×60 cm. Kunstmuseum, Basel.

The Saint-Martin Canal. 1906-07. Oil on canvas, 61 × 73 cm.
Private collection.

blues, and the white of the canvas shows through in bands
or streaks of varying breadth, giving the work greater
lightness and serenity. Sometimes, however, movement
prevails over stillness: the trees and their shadows in one
Landscape near L'Estaque froth and foam in strips and
swirls of pleasant pinks, blues, and mauves. But was this
sort of Fauvism not in danger of becoming merely a
harmonious interplay of patches of color gaily scattered
over the canvas? Was there not something in it of that
capricious, nerveless beauty for which the Fauvists had
reproached the Impressionists, without stopping to
consider that their own work was an extreme consequence
of the same thing? There was no danger of this happening
in Braque's case: this particular Fauve may have been
quiet, but he was not a dreamer lost in the clouds. The
construction of his pictures had been one of his principal
concerns since his earliest works; this is evident in *The
Saint-Martin Canal*, in which the reduction in the depth
of the perspective causes the houses and their reflections
to form a geometrical assemblage worthy of the Cubist
pictures that were to come. This was, moreover, a lesson
on which Braque had meditated even before working at
L'Estaque, one he had learnt from a painter who had just
attained a certain reputation among his colleagues and who
was to die that same year: Paul Cézanne.

THE LESSON OF CÉZANNE

If Cézanne's death marked the end of one era in painting,
it likewise meant the beginning of another. "Anybody who
understands Cézanne has a premonition of Cubism," was
the peremptory verdict of Gleizes and Metzinger in their
book on the new movement, *Du cubisme* (1912). "That
vast, seething undulation which is endlessly repeated in
the work of the Impressionists—not having to yield place
to anything else—is immobilized and solidified in that
of Cézanne," André Lhote was to write (*Les invariants
plastiques*, 1920). Certain versions of Braque's *Landscape
near L'Estaque* bring out very well this confrontation of
two conceptions which Braque appears to have been
attempting to bring together: from a fleecy mass of
greenery underlined by vigorously curving arcs of violet,
blue, or dark green (all of which is the heritage of Impressionism in the revised and corrected edition of the Fauvists)
we see emerging here and there geometrical solids that are
houses; these houses finally prevail over everything else

and stand out from the crest of the mountain, which
is in turn outlined against the sky. Braque's painter
colleagues and the critics were not yet speaking of "little
cubes" or "cubism" in relation to his works, as they would
be less than two years later, for the color in these pictures
is still predominant and makes them unmistakably Fauvist.
It is quite clear that Braque, although he was the last of
the Fauves, was by no means the least.

Braque was back in Paris by February 1970, but he
returned to the Midi the following summer, staying first
at La Ciotat and later at L'Estaque again. Years later he
was to explain to Jean Paulhan how this second stay had
differed from the first: "The first year it was a matter of
pure enthusiasm, the astonishment of a Parisian discov-
ering the Midi. The second year it had already changed.
I should have had to go as far as Senegal. Enthusiasm
cannot be counted on for longer than ten months" (J.
Paulhan, *Braque le patron*). And this change is reflected
in the pictures he painted. One of the most characteristic
is the *View of L'Estaque from the Hotel Mistral*. Here
there is no longer any confusion of forms; a single
conception prevails and geometrizes into angles, straight
lines, and circles the trees and the houses; the very composition of the picture, with its right-angled lines, almost
amounts to a manifesto; the terrace is a regular band
occupying the lowest quarter of the picture, while the
upper three-quarters is perpendicularly cut by three trees
that divide the space of the background into four parts—if
one can still speak of foregrounds and backgrounds, for
the multiple perspectives governing the elements of the
picture almost succeed in maintaining the whole in two
dimensions—like a stage set of shapes without relief, in
which the foreground and background signify depth
without providing the least illusion of such depth. It
was a question, as Braque was later to say, "of a new
conception of space. I was saying goodbye to the vanishing
point. And in order to avoid a projection into infinity I
put superimposed planes within a short distance: to make
it clear that the things are in front of one another rather
than arranged in the space. Cézanne had thought a lot
about this. We need only compare his landscapes with
Corot's, for instance, to see that it is no longer a question
of distance, that after him there is no longer any infinite."
(Interview with Jacques Lassaigne, 1961, included in the
catalogue of the exhibition *Les Cubistes*, Bordeaux-Paris,
1973). The light and color so dear to the Impressionists
and the Fauves have here given place to the preoccupation
with *space*, the crucial subject of reflection for the Cubists.
True, the color is still there—totally subjective and yet less
vivid, I should point out—but now it is no longer the color
that catches the viewer's eye. Having gone as far as
possible with chromatic Fauvism, Braque had discovered
that color had given all it could and that now he had to
work on the structure of the space and the objects in his
pictures—in other words, to move away from Fauvism.
At this point he had not yet really reached the fully
Cézanne-inspired period of Cubism, but he could no
longer be said to belong to the Fauvists proper; Matisse
and Derain, for instance, though not unacquainted with
the work of the great master of Aix-en-Provence, had
never thought of embarking on any systematic application
of his discoveries. With a canvas like the *View of
L'Estaque from the Hotel Mistral*, Braque had taken a
still more decisive step in the direction of Cubism,
although it was one that Cézanne would almost certainly
not have sanctioned: the emancipation of the model. From
the starting-point of a model still taken from the real
world, the painter was now going to reorganize everything
to suit his own purposes by working the painting out in
his studio. In the above case he arranged the elements in

a series of perpendiculars, remodelling and schematizing the trees and houses in firmly enclosed geometrical forms that were all the more simple inasmuch as he did not give them any effect of relief. Since the color no longer determined the form, as it had during his Fauvist period, it naturally lost a great deal of its former importance. With regard to this transition from Fauvism to Cubism, Braque was later to say: "The process was almost automatic. I realized one day that I could go back over the same motif for as long as I liked. I no longer needed the sun, for I carried my own light with me. There was one danger, however: I very nearly found myself slipping into monochrome" (J. Paulhan, *Braque le patron*). This tendency to monochrome, not yet evident in the 1907 works, was to be noticeable the following year. But let us not leap too far ahead, for before 1908 we find an important event, which has furnished occasion for a great deal of theorizing.

First, however, I should like to make a brief digression. I am well aware that I am upsetting habitual attitudes by challenging the more or less clear-cut division which is usually drawn between Fauvism and Cubirm—and which has the advantage of simplifying things considerably by regarding Cubism as an independent movement with precisely defined origins. Until recently everything seemed quite clear: Picasso painted *Les demoiselles d'Avignon*, Braque imitated him with the *Large Nude*—and Cubism was ready to begin. For some time now, however, this assumption has seemed rather less certain. In establishing a direct connection between Fauvism and Cubism, with Cézanne and then Matisse as the links, I have at least the excuse of not being the first; for Jean Laude (*Braque: le Cubisme*, in the catalogue of the exhibition at the Maeght Foundation in 1982) had already posed this question in the plainest terms. A point to be noted, incidentally, is that on at least two occasions Guillaume Apollinaire described Fauvism as "the prelude to Cubism" (*Les peintres cubistes*, 1913). Admittedly, no more attention was paid to him than if he had been guilty of a mere blunder or a facilely journalistic approach to the question. But Apollinaire had known and defended the painting confraternity for long enough to be accorded some degree of credit, which caused Jean Laude to exclaim: "Are we to understand that, contrary to an opinion that is still widely propagated and believed today, the poet did not consider *Les demoiselles d'Avignon* to be the origin of Cubism? Or did he, perhaps, see in what was called Cubism the convergence of two lines of research which were worked out in different places before joining up and fertilizing each other?" In other words, while Picasso came to Cubism from a succession of different experiences which he synthesized in *Les demoiselles d'Avignon*, Braque came straight from Fauvism, albeit a Fauvism gradually modified by this study of Cézanne. And, after all, Robert Delaunay, Jean Metzinger, Auguste Herbin and quite a few others were likewise to come from Fauvism—or, at least, from Divisionism.

In the early autumn of 1907 two events occurred that were undeniably important for Braque, but which we should be careful to interpret properly. The first was a series of public celebrations in connection with Cézanne, commemorating the first anniversary of his death: a retrospective at the Salon d'automne, an exhibition of his watercolors at the Galerie Bernheim Jeune, and the publication of his letters to Émile Bernard, to which future historians were to pay such great attention—although, even supposing that they read them at the time, painters like Matisse, Derain, Braque, and even Picasso had not awaited their publication to engage in speculation on the work of Cézanne. Braque—who as we have seen was in the middle of his experiments with Cézanne's ideas and was not yet prepared to give them up—must surely have seen those exhibitions and felt his interest in Cézanne strengthened. The second, and more important, of these two events was Braque's meeting with Picasso, to whose studio he had been taken by Apollinaire; Picasso was then just finishing his great picture *Les demoiselles d'Avignon*. Many years later, certain people—whether or not they were eyewitnesses of this meeting of which Apollinaire himself tells us nothing—were to write that Braque had been stupefied, quite disconcerted, by Picasso's new work. Fair enough; one can quite easily imagine it. It is later on that everything gets more complicated. In the late autumn of 1907, Braque began to paint his *Large Nude* (also known as the *Large Bather*), on which he worked all through the winter. To anyone who had not studied the evolution of Braque's painting throughout the preceding months of 1907, this work might well seem unexpected enough. Thus it was generally concluded that its novelty could only have originated in Picasso's picture, and that is the version that has been accredited by a whole generation of critics, most of them of the Anglo-Saxon persuasion (John Russell, Douglas Cooper, Guy Habasque, and even John Golding, who is usually so careful to give every man his due). After that there was no doubt in anybody's mind. "Braque may at first have been totally disconcerted by *Les demoiselles d'Avignon*; but he was also, and to no less a degree, stimulated by that picture. The result was his *Large Bather*, or *Large Nude*.... His indebtedness to Picasso is evident." (J. Golding, *Cubism, a History and Analysis, 1907-1914*, 1959); or again: "The effect of the *Demoiselles* on Braque was to make him renounce Fauvism and decide to follow Picasso.... Braque's debt to Picasso is explicit." (D. Cooper, *The Cubist Epoch*, 1971). But history written a posteriori on a basis of anecdotes recalled many years later can hardly prevail over the factual evidence that remains, which is the pictures themselves.

The *Large Nude* represents an important milestone on the way that Braque set out on in the course of his second stay in the Midi. The coloring has again been considerably muted, confined as it is to ochres and greens without the slightest hint of harshness; the firmly enclosed forms are still simplified, and the flattening that we have already seen in the 1907 Fauve pictures is even more accentuated—to such a point, indeed, that the female body is distorted as though it had been crushed. The originality of this nude lies in the fact that the figure is not standing but lying down and seen from above; the viewer is in the position of somebody looking down perpendicularly at a character lying on a green cloth spread on the ground. The main novelty in the treatment of the subject is not so much the reduction of the colors as the way in which they are applied: by vigorous brushstrokes, always more or less oblique, and with a certain turbulence hitherto almost unknown in Braque. It was the most ambitious picture he had attempted so far; doubtless he too wished to try his hand at larger formats, as had his older Fauvist confrères, Picasso, and so many others.

What could Braque have really taken from *Les demoiselles d'Avignon*? The subject, and its distortions? But nudes and bathers, after all, are as old as painting itself; and as for the distortions, already evident in Cézanne's *Bather*, they were *de rigueur* in the Fauvist nudes, in the bathers depicted by Derain or Vlaminck, and in the numerous nudes painted by Matisse; in fact the leg and the foot in the *Large Nude* are remarkably similar to the leg and the foot in that *Blue Nude* that Matisse had painted and exhibited in 1907. In that same year Braque had already painted *Seated Nude Seen from Behind*, in which the back seen slantwise was already singularly distorted. It is true that the face in the *Large Nude* reminds one of a mask, but it does not resemble any of the faces in the *Demoiselles*; it is even more schematic, though not to such an extent as the face in Vlaminck's *Bathers* (1907); the eyes, understandably closed since the character is lying down, not standing, give a rather empty, dead impression, unlike those in the *Demoiselles*. The distortions of Braque's nude are the effect of a flattening and twisting of the figure, as though to let us see it simultaneously from different angles, but they constitute a coherent ensemble, whereas Picasso's five angular, naked women form a barbaric, disparate group in which each one is given a different treatment—which makes them fascinating. To tell the truth, the languid movement of the *Large Nude* is more reminiscent of another picture by Picasso, the *Nude with Draperies* (1907), in which a sort of angular black Venus simpers at us with lowered eyes, one hand behind her head and the other resting on a console. Many critics have emphasized the austerity of the colors in Braque's picture, but in the *Demoiselles*, despite the predominance of ochre and faded pink, the blue and the reds still make their presence felt. And whereas the background in the *Demoiselles*—like the picture as a whole—is tormented with pointed forms and contrasting colors, the *Large Nude* lies on a monochrome background of ill-defined, barely discernible forms, the type of vague background already to be found in Braque's work in the *Seated Nude Seen from Behind*. How can anyone see similarities between two such different works as *Les demoiselles d'Avignon* and the *Large Nude*? I am surely not disputing the supremacy accorded to Picasso in twentieth-century art by saying that Braque would have reached the goal he was heading for in 1908 without any help from the *Demoiselles d'Avignon*; at most his progress would have been encouraged, perhaps even accelerated by it. The two artists were to have sufficient occasion to exchange ideas in the years that followed, were to recognize each other's merits sufficiently, without there being any need to begin any account of their relationship with a "debt." Besides, these notions of indebtedness seem rather petty when we consider those words of Matisse so justly recalled by Pierre Descargues with regard to those precedences and priorities with which critics short of arguments are fond of playing. Speaking of the first Cubist picture (which according to him appears to have been painted by Braque), Matisse said: "I saw the picture in the studio rented by Picasso, who was discussing it with some friends of his.... At that time we were not imprisoned in uniforms, and any daring or novelty that could be found in a friend's picture belonged to us all."

Braque and Picasso soon realized that they had much to learn from each other; despite—or perhaps because of—differences of training and temperament, they were to become close friends, the most remarkable pair in modern art, seeing each other every day, taking their holidays together until they were separated by the War. "...We had daily exchanges of ideas, each tried out the other's ideas, we compared our repective works." (Interview with Jacques Lassaigne, 1961); "We were rather like mountaineers on the same rope.... We both worked a great deal.... We were no longer interested in museums. We used to go to exhibitions, but not so often as is generally believed. Above all, we were enormously absorbed" (Interview with Dora Vallier). It is Braque who is speaking here, but it might just as easily be Picasso. Similarly, from now on, even if I am dealing with Braque's work, I will not try to discriminate precisely what may have come from one rather than the other. It is only the works that count.

STILL CÉZANNE

Picasso and Braque stimulated each other, and they were greatly helped by the faith and support of poet friends such as Max Jacob and, above all, Guillaume Apollinaire. They all formed a merry little band about which a great many stories have been told. But they worked hard and thought a lot, too. Apollinaire saw very clearly the direction in which Braque's work was going and how, after giving up Fauvism, he had gradually given himself up to an ideal that was less extroverted, not as concerned with color as with a well-thought-out composition. In the spring of 1908—possibly apropos of the *Large Nude*, since he mentions a "large composition"—Apollinaire stressed the novelty of the work in the contemporary art scene and the problems of composition with which the painter was constantly concerned. "We need not dwell on the summary expression of this composition, but we must acknowledge that M. Braque has faultlessly accomplished his purpose of constructing. The science of construction confronts the painter with many problems not yet resolved, and M. Braque valiantly faces some of these. This is simply a rather stormy stage in this painter's proud ascent.... *(La revue des Lettres et des Arts*, 1st May 1908). This "purpose of constructing" was to appear even more plainly in the pictures Braque painted at this time in L'Estaque, to which he had returned for a second stay, this time in the company of Raoul Dufy.

Why L'Estaque again? For convenience, because he had got used to it? But again, why, if the years before he had already lost all interest in painting from life in the open air, if the bright light and vivid colors that had fascinated him in 1906 had by now lost all their relevance to his intentions? It was probably a question of fidelity to Cézanne, a fascination with that master's work, that led him back to the Midi; and even more probably a desire to compare his new experiments with those earlier ones, as though he wished in this way to maintain a stricter

Houses at L'Estaque. 1908. Oil on canvas, 73 × 60 cm. Kunstmuseum, Bern.

control over his advance in the direction of something as yet undefined, beyond Cézanne. It was on that account, undoubtedly, that he returned to themes he had already painted the previous year, such as *The Viaduct at L'Estaque* or *Terrace of the Hotel Mistral*. The new works did not resemble the old ones much, with their colors now so few and their perspective violently shaken up. It was as though the painter, now working in his studio, could only be content with souvenirs, rearranged to suit his taste, of what he could have before his eyes outside that studio.

Of the pictures of this period *The Viaduct at L'Estaque* is the one that comes closest to a conventional view. In its forms and colors, however, one immediately notices something that is not "natural" (but "nature does not exist," Pierre Reverdy was to say, in the very book, so charmingly entitled *Une aventure méthodique*, that he devoted to Braque's work in 1950). In front of a horizon crossed by the arches of the viaduct, and deprived of any sort of calm by the nervous brushwork, we have an interlocking of geometrical solids that are houses—recognizable as such by the shape of their roofs rather than by their almost nonexistent doors and windows. There were already several vanishing points in the arches of the viaduct, but there are far more in the houses: not only does their general mass have quite a few, but sometimes a single house has several of its own; the one whose façade confronts us, for instance, is also visible right along one of its sides, and a good many other twists are given to the traditional idea of perspective. The coloring of the picture is equally surprising, for it is hardly anything more than a variation on two colors: ochre and a sort of emerald tone with more or less green, more or less blue, according to whether it is applied to the sky or to the vegetation. These peculiarities were to be accentuated in other pictures. The *Houses in L'Estaque*, which is in the Kunstmuseum in Bern, is nothing but a jumble of hard-edged crystals that only remind us of houses because a tree trunk and some leafless branches in the foreground suggest that this picture is a landscape. These were the "little cubes," mockingly referred to at the first exhibition of these pictures, that were to give Cubism its name. In the *Landscape near L'Estaque* in the Basel Kunstmuseum the reading was to become even more subtle, for in this picture the geometrical forms are so thoroughly jumbled that it is difficult to see any houses in it, except for a little group paradoxically lost in the distance into which the tree itself merges in defiance of either scale or logic, since its base appears in transparency through a house. The green-ochre duality that is still clear in *Houses in L'Estaque* tends to disappear and leave the field to a generalized blue-green, the ochre being thrown overboard as though in the interests of monochrome. Here more than elsewhere one senses *the absence of any source of light*; there is no longer any sun; *the objects radiate their own light*. The pictures are now a world without a horizon, closed in on itself, generating itself, outside all reality.

We have now entered what is called the "Cézanne" period of Cubism (Picasso, who had in turn also been seized by a great interest in Cézanne, was working along the same lines in his studio in the Rue-aux-Bois). Speaking of the research he had done during his third stay in the Midi, Braque was later to say: "I had to find other means for my nature.... When one thinks about it, that changes the color of a thing.... I had been impressed by Cézanne, by those pictures of his I had seen at Vollard's gallery; I felt that there was something more secret in that painting" (Interview with Dora Vallier).

Braque had now grasped all that he had to learn from Cézanne. Though always working scrupulously from life, Cézanne had instinctively done a number of things which the nascent Cubist movement was to take up again on its own account: "Cézanne's research on perspective discovered by its fidelity to phenomena all that the new science of psychology was to formulate. Perspective as experienced through our perception is not the same as geometrical or photographic perspective." In Cézanne, Maurice Merleau-Ponty goes on to say, "the object is no longer covered with reflections, lost in its relationship with the air or with other objects; it seems to be dimly lit from the interior, with the light emanating from it, and the resultant impression is one of solidity and materiality.... We must conclude, therefore, that he wished to return to the object without abandoning the Impressionist aesthetic that took its models from nature" (M. Merleau-Ponty, *Sens et Nonsens*). Braque himself was fond of saying that "the object is poetry"; in fact it is observable in his work that the objects have an inner light of their own—whether they be the houses in L'Estaque or the musical instruments he was to paint at a later stage. But Braque rejected the Impressionist aesthetic, with its interplay of colors and reflections; at the same time he rejected nature and painting from life as being no more than a pretext by which, unlike Cézanne, he did not feel himself to be bound. "Working from nature is improvizing," Braque was to say scornfully; for art, in his opinion, is not improvized but constructed.

Francis Ponge, in his *Le peintre à l'étude*, contributes a singular reflection: "Braque says that after the age of twenty-five one ceases to see." By this he meant, referring to psychology, that after 1907 he had seen enough, had sufficiently studied the outside world (he said that he had given up visiting museums in that year and went to very few exhibitions) to be able to dispense with it in his art and to work on the basis of his own vision of things. In future he was to give each picture the form and color that suited it according to the rules of the picture, not according to the old rules of perpective or the new rules of Impressionist or Neo-Impressionist coloring. His rules of the picture at that time were austere, and they were to remain so for several years: a strict limitation of the colors combined with maximum simplification of the forms. Two aphorisms published in 1917, in his friend Reverdy's review, *Nord-Sud*, help to explain the *raison d'être* of these restraints: "Limiting the means gives the style, engenders the new form and gives an impulse to creation," and "It is often limited means that make the charm and the force of primary paintings. Extension, on the contrary, leads the arts to decadence."

There can be no doubt that Braque and his friend Picasso felt positively stimulated by the restraints they imposed on themselves. Even within a restricted scope there is always some way of exercizing the imagination. Consider, for instance, the enormous freedom with which the musical instruments painted in Paris are treated; as in the houses at L'Estaque, we find few colors and a very simple contrast between circular and angular forms, but a great diversity of approach; the distortions are such that with the contradictions among the shadows there is no longer any question of perspective: the chassis of the mandola and the horn of the clarinet are flattened on the canvas, but the concertina and the musical scores, on the other hand, seem to rise up in the air against all the laws of logic or gravity.

The reaction to such a challenge was not long in coming. When Braque presented his pictures to the 1908 Salon d'automne, the committee rejected them; at that time all the garishly colored whims of the Fauvists were permitted, since they did not call into question that logic and conception of the world that Braque's canvases so foolishly defied. Fortunately, Braque had met a young dealer, D. H. Kahnweiler, who took the risk of organizing Braque's first one-man show, with a catalogue prefaced by his friend Apollinaire. The poet's preface claimed that this rejection of the external world in its conventional representations was the painter's greatest merit, which evaluation shows considerable penetration, arriving so long before the development of the movement in painting that was to come: "Drawing from deep down in himself the elements of the synthetic motifs that they represent, he has become a creative artist. He no longer owes anything to the world around him. His spirit has deliberately brought about the twilight of reality, and now we may see him working out, within himself and in the external world, a universal renaissance."

What admirable prescience! Cubism was in fact to be a renaissance—and even, as Apollinaire later wrote, a "revolution." But not everybody shared the poet's enthusiasm. There was also scepticism, laughter, a lot of talk about "cubism," so that the word survived. It hardly mattered; something new had been revealed to the public for the first time in 1908, and for its most attentive members this was, as Marcel Duchamp was to say, "the signpost pointing to the new road" (*Catalogue of the "Societé Anonyme,"* 1943).

ANALYTICAL CUBISM

The year 1909 was to be less characteristic, perhaps, and not so coherent as 1908, but it was a pivotal year of great importance. Braque's interest in landscape continued, but now he sought to broaden its possibilities. He worked in the Île-de-France and in Normandy. *The Castle of La Roche-Guyon* is still in the line of his Cézanne-inspired research at L'Estaque, but the cones, cylinders, and cubes of his contructions have already gone beyond their models, while at the same time the picture has abandoned any attempt at depth, for the painter's sole intention is to produce a harmony of forms and the opposition of ochre and green on a two-dimensional surface. His *Port in Normandy*, though betraying no greater a concern for depth, is presented in quite a different fashion, one that has come a long way from Cézanne: the subject does not disappear as the result of a great schematizing effect, but because the ensemble is broken up into planes of color and the same treatment is given to all the elements: the ships have the same structure of planes and the same colors (for this time the picture, oddly enough, is polychromatic) as the sky, the quays, or the reflections in the sea. The whole space of the picture has solidified in a mosaic of overlapping and interpenetrating planes, though no one detail of sky, earth, or water can be isolated from the rest of the context. The picture presents itself as a whole, not as an assembly of independent elements. At this stage of the analysis of the subject the landscape here is still easily discernable in this mosaic of colors—not so much on account of the circumscribed forms (ships, lighthouses) as because of the diversified colors. Such a breaking up of the painted surface into multiple planes in order to give an idea of the space, to make it almost palpable, was to be a characteristic of what later came to be called analytical Cubism. For the moment the painter had not got that far; he was working in several directions: landscape, still life (in which he was becoming decidedly more interested), and, though still more occasionally, portraiture.

Although he had said that he was interested in the masks of Negro art, Braque was not to assimilate much from them in his own work. The 1909 *Woman's Head*, interesting for the way its lights and shades so arbitrarily

Woman's Head. 1909. Oil on canvas, 41 × 33 cm. Musée d'Art Moderne de la Ville de Paris.

divide the face into geometrical planes, owes nothing to Negro art, nor even to the very lively portraits Picasso was painting at the time. Picasso's portraits are always recognizable despite all the breaking up—unlike this portrait, which is treated as an inanimate object without any personality. To tell the truth, Braque was not particularly interested in the portrait as a genre, and he very soon acknowledged this: "I had painted a great many portraits in my youth, almost all of them since destroyed. But this had never really interested me, and even when I painted figures, during the period of our Cubist research, I regarded them as still lifes. Picasso, on the contrary, has always painted real portraits" (Interview, already quoted, with Jacques Lassaigne). Even in 1908, in his review of the exhibition at Kahnweiler's gallery, one critic had seen this and had written: "Nobody has paid less attention to psychology that he has; and I would say that he is as much moved by a stone as by a face" (Charles Morice, *Mercure de France,* 16 Decembre 1908). He cannot have known how right he was. In this portrait the female face is treated in exactly the same prismatic fashion, no more and no less, as a jug or pitcher of the same period. Throughout his career, Braque never confused art with psychology or sentimentalism, with which it has nothing to do. Reverdy, for his part, was to recall that poetry does not reside in either life or things, but in what one makes of them. Braque was to concentrate on what he thought was most likely to arouse poetry. Merely remarking that he preferred still life to portraiture does not take us very far; in a work of art it is not so much the subject that counts as the result.

While the compositions of his "Cézanne" period still followed the general outline of whatever fragment of reality (a landscape, a musical instrument) served as their pretext, those of the analytical period were to break away from such reality. In his notes Braque was to write: "One should not imitate what one wishes to believe," to which he at once added: "In art there can be no effect without twisting the truth." The fact is that the truth of art is not the pragmatic truth that an academic vision of things prefers to retain. Far from being an abstract art, Cubism aimed at better *grasping* reality in all its aspects, not according to what is seen by the camera or the impressionist eye, but according to what the painter knows of it, from a point of view that is more alive, no longer static. Cubism mistrusted an oversimple approach ("The senses deform, the spirit forms," we find in another of Braque's notes), and it was in this sense that the Cubists willingly presented themselves as *realists*. This point was insisted on, not only by the poets (Apollinaire, Salmon, Reverdy, Cendrars) who wrote about this movement but also by the painters themselves. Fernand Léger, for instance, wrote: "The realistic value of a work is totally independent of any imitative quality.... Pictorial realism is the simultaneous organization of three great plastic qualities: the Lines, the Forms, and the Colors" (*Les origines de la peinture et sa valeur représentative*, 1913).

The lighting (more so in the case of artificial lighting in the studio) tends to distort quite as much as our mental habit of picturing objects to ourselves according to established conventions more or less modified by psychology. Cézanne had intuitively felt this, but without much consequence to his work, apart from some alterations of perspective; we cannot see the Cubism of Braque and Picasso as simply descending from Cézanne, insofar as the master of Aix-en-Provence would not have contemplated, still less approved, such a development if he had lived to see it. "Traditional perspective did not satisfy me," Braque was later to say. "Mechanized as it is, it never gives the full possession of things" (In a conversation with Jean Leymarie, 1961). Rejecting the single viewpoint of photography or of perspective as imposed since the Renaissance, "the full possession of things" entails grasping them from different angles, that is to say installing them in *duration*; hence some writers—among them Apollinaire, Metzinger, and Maurice Raynal—were to invoke the "fourth dimension" in explaining Cubist painting. A little later the Futurist painters in Italy were in turn to invoke duration, but in order to express movement, dynamism: while the object moves in front of the Futurist painter, in Cubism it is the painter who moves in front of the object. Whether it be a character or a guitar, it is caught at once frontally and in profile, or from intermediate angles.

Towards the end of 1909, Braque began work on two pictures intended to form a pair and in an oblong format that was rather unusual, but for which he was to retain a certain affection: *Piano and Mandola* and *Violin and Palette*. Except for the upper right-hand corner of the second picture, the whole surface of each of these canvases is a jigsaw of facets in restrained colors, a procedure we have already found in his *Port in Normandy*. The painter no longer follows the volumes at all; he shows us the objects from a multitude of angles intersecting and blocking each other. The piano, for instance, is seen from the side, but also from above, since the keys are quite visible; and yet the keys are also seen face-on, for we can see their ends, etc. The painter has reconstructed his subject in accordance with clear-cut angles that permit no fuzziness on the canvas. In the works of the Impressionists the object was lost in a haze of color and light, a representation that seemed too vague, too passive to the eyes of painters like Braque and Picasso. Wyndham Lewis summed it up in a phrase: "The Cubist movement, or the movement of which Braque's are the key works, is an extremely intense reaction aimed at finding the Constructive and the Inventive in painting, a reaction appearing right in the middle of the massive dogmatism of French Impressionism" (*The Athenaeum*, January 1920). And

Apollinaire exclaimed: "To the *silhouette* of the Impressionists Georges Braque opposes the *profile*" (*L'Europe nouvelle*, 10 August 1918). In these Cubist canvases, which are on the contrary extremely precise, the object is shattered into fragments because it is analyzed from very close up and from a variable viewpoint. The painter wants to show more than can be caught by the ordinary eye; in order to prevent the viewer from getting quite lost, we see him moving towards a system of *signs*, which were to become increasingly important as he moved in the direction of a more abstract Cubism. Even here a few lines above a circle are enough to suggest a stringed instrument, while one of two inverted S's signify sound-holes, and therefore a violin. From that point on, the fragmenting may be carried very far indeed, as may be seen in *Still Life with Metronome*, painted in 1910, or in the 1911 *Violin*. There is, however, something very disturbing, and as yet undiscussed, in the upper part of *Violin and Palette*: against the background of a curtain, a conventionally drawn palette is hung from a *trompe-l'œil* nail that casts its shadow on the canvas! One might perhaps believe that this nail, so utterly contradictory of the principles that the painter had established for himself, is a sort of joke intended to remind us that the canvas is an object that does not attempt to deceive us and that we can hang from a point, can indeed nail to a wall; or here to affirm that painting is less abstract than music. Beyond a humorous intention, which should certainly not be excluded, there is a more serious *raison d'être* for this nail, which is the height of the anecdotal, and all the more so since it reappears in two other canvases of the same period. Among those who have written about this detail, John Golding proposes this explanation: "Particularly anxious to maintain contact with reality, Braque had more or less consciously realized that at that moment Cubism could only evolve in the direction of abstraction, and this illusionistic nail may be a sort of manifesto of the movement's realistic intentions" (*op. cit.*, 1959). Perhaps we may remember this explanation better if we think of an ironical note by Braque himself: "I have found painting ideal for hanging my ideas from a nail: that permits one to change them and avoid fixed ideas."

In this analytical style Braque also painted some very fine landscapes: *The Rio Tinto Works at L'Estaque*— for he had, indeed, gone back yet again to these scenes of his earlier experiences—and *The Sacré-Coeur*, which he could see, at some distance, from his studio in Montmartre. Since the architecture of the Sacré Coeur is familiar to everybody, the artist needs only to give a sketchy outline of the two domes for us to recognize immediately, knowing the picture's title, the famous church in Montmartre. Without this familiarity with the building, and without the title, we would find the canvas impenetrable (many critics, indeed, like to apply the term "hermetic Cubism" to the paintings or engravings of this period). But it would not matter very much, for we would still have a work in which the ochre, brown, and blue planes are marvellously harmonized. Since then abstract painting has accustomed us to doing without any reference to a possible reality. But in 1910 neither Braque nor Picasso wanted to take this plunge, as Kandinsky and Mondrian were to. It may have been this fear of being no longer able to keep any sign of reality that led Braque to give up landscape painting in 1911; he was not to return to this genre until many years later.

For a character, or a still life with familiar objects, a few strokes are sufficient to retain reality. In *Woman with Mandolin* (1910) the line of an arm and a hand are enough for the whole character, a circle and a few strokes enough for the instrument. A movement of ascending lines suggests the contours of a bust surmounted by what would seem to be a skull rather than a face. Indeed, since the colors are muted and always arranged in horizontal brushstrokes, what strikes one most of all is the perfect composition, the tracery of ascending lines on a background of horizontal lines. The composed aspect of the work is accentuated by its oval form, a sort of tondo revived by Braque and one he was often to use. Unlike Fauvism, Cubism is not structured by the color but by the line, the stroke. Even when the subject is shattered, the drawing is always unostentatiously precise. Is it not possible that the Cubists wanted to recover the clean austerity of drawing that had been lost after Ingres (a painter the Cubists were to appreciate greatly)? We should remember that many of the Cubists were great engravers; Jacques Villon and Louis Marcoussis, for instance, spent most of their time on this branch of their art; and, though not approaching the vast abundance of Picasso's, Braque's output of engravings was considerable.

STENCILED LETTERS

A structure of ascending lines on a background of horizontal lines is often found again in the hermetic works painted in 1911. Of particular importance is *The Portuguese*. Painted during the summer in Céret, where Braque had gone to work in the company of Picasso, this work is supposed to have been inspired by a musician Braque met in Marseilles, though it is also said to be a portrait of the painter Souza-Cardoso, with whom Braque had become acquainted; but it hardly matters. The great novelty of this picture is the presence of letters and numerals stenciled onto the canvas, a commonplace technique for a former painter and decorator like Braque, but quite unusual in an easel painting. What are these characters supposed to represent in the context of the picture? An advertisement or a poster partially perceived,

at the same time as the form of the musician, or through the reflections of a shop window. The fragment *D BAL* is supposed by some to be the remains of GRAND BAL, and this would be confirmed by the inscription *0,40*, which could be the price of a ticket, and the presence of the guitarist—unless, of course, the letters are what is left of *POD BAL*, that is, nothing, in accordance with a formula that was to appeal to Marcel Duchamp, for a facetious spirit soon presided over these inscriptions, which from now on were to be a sign of Cubism. But whether they were proper names (Socrate, Bach), fragments of posters (Concert, Bal), commercial labels (Vieux marc, Ale), names of newspapers (*L'Écho d'Athènes, Le quotidien du Midi*), or even cut-out fragments of text, how could they have had any but a strictly plastic function, simply for their forms and colors? Unlike the *trompe-l'œil* nail, which created a localized impression of depth, these stenciled inscriptions indicated the total absence of depth of the painted surface, but likewise underlined at the same time the picture's aspect as an object, something manufactured. These signs so artlessly reproduced are fragments of reality that have not been transposed. Braque later explained them as follows: "Still wishing to approach a reality as closely as possible, in 1911 I introduced letters in my pictures. They were forms in which there was nothing to distort since, being flat, the letters were outside space and their presence in the picture, by contrast, made it possible to distinguish the objects situated in the space from those that were outside the space" (Interview with Dora Vallier). As an autonomous flat object made by such an impersonal method as the stencil, and no longer a "work of art," produced by an artist's talent and imagination, the picture was coming closer to the manufactured object (before very long Duchamp was to introduce his *ready-mades*, but first there was to be the intermediate period of the papiers collés). A certain impersonality ensued in the works, or so at least it was thought, and all the more so because it was during this period of hermetic Cubism and papiers collés that the works of Braque and Picasso most resembled each other—"there was a moment when we had difficulty in recognizing our own canvases" (Interview with Dora Vallier)—and to such an extent, Paulhan was to say, "that the experts were frequently confused and the painters themselves were not always able to draw a distinction in their common output between their respective works" (*La peinture cubiste*). It is an exaggerated remark, but not without significance. But let us listen to Braque himself again: "I considered that there was no need for the painter's *person* to appear and that, consequently, the pictures should be anonymous. It was I who decided that the canvases ought not be signed, and for some time Picasso did the same. Seeing that anybody could do the same things as myself, I thought that there was no difference between the pictures and that there was no need to sign them. Later I realized that all of that was not true and I began to sign my convases again. Besides, Picasso had also started to sign his work again" (Interview with Dora Vallier). The stenciled letters were recognized at once by Picasso as an interesting process, as was the use of the "comb" that Braque suggested to him at this time. The "comb" is a tool used by painters and decorators for imitating the streaking of marble or the grain of wood; and the mechanical aspect of its use, like the visible "false" appearance of the result obtained, tends to reinforce still more the impersonality of the works in which it features. Examples of this are the 1911 *"Waltz" Still Life*, the 1912 *Fruit Dish*, and the 1914 *Still Life with Grapes*. Now that Braque had started out in this direction, the discovery of collage and papiers collés could not be long in coming.

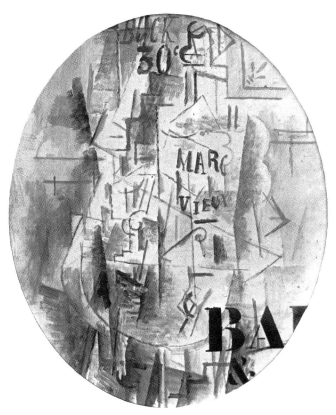

The Bottle of Old Marc. 1912. Oil on canvas, 55 × 46 cm. Private collection.

Before studying those developments, however, it might be useful to take our bearings. Coming by different routes, then, Braque and Picasso had finally converged; from 1908 on they had worked together, creating a new art that has come to be called Cubism, and regarding which the task of sorting out the respective contributions of the two and the influence of each on the other has been (and will be for a long time yet) an absorbing investigation if we are trying to reconstitute a historic development, but a rather futile academic exercise if we are concerned with beauty and an aesthetic emotion unconnected with names or personalities—no point in signing the canvases, as Braque was to say. Their revolution was carried out against the loss of form and construction in Impressionism, but no less so against the extroverted color of the Fauves, whether dazzling as in Derain or more restrained as in Marquet. There is hardly any set of themes that they did not submit to reconsideration. Social, historical, religious, or mythological painting, and even that allegorical painting to which Matisse had shown some attachment: none of these approaches was retained. At most, at the beginning of the adventure some traces of previous styles remain in Picasso's work, such as the 1908 *Dryad* or even *Les demoiselles d'Avignon*, which is a theme from Toulouse-Lautrec. It is significant that Braque's *Large Nude* was first conceived as a bather in a landscape. Fernand Léger was to say, with a shrug of his shoulders, in 1913: "I really wonder what all these more or less historical or dramatic pictures in the French Salons hope to achieve in competition with the first cinema screen to present itself" (*Les origines de la peinture et sa valeur représentative*). The innovations of technology, mechanization, speed, and the new processes for recording images and sounds had changed man's vision of the world; the painters were well aware of this and the most farsighted among them very soon assimilated the fact in their canvases. The discoveries of Cubism were corroborated by those of science: Einstein proved that matter was not what people thought it to be; Bergson and Freud revealed stranger depths in man than anybody had believed possible. Everything became uncertain, everything had to be reconsidered. It is symptomatic that Braque should have chosen, even more decidedly than Picasso, a set of themes at once anti-romantic and more suited to reflection; after giving up landscape painting in 1911, he was to retain only the human figure (but not the too-anecdotal genre of portraiture) and, above all, still life. A more meditative art, which lends itself to introspective thought processes, still life was always to remain Braque's favorite mode of expression: in it the object is thought out for the work, then rethought in all its aspects beyond the traditional systems of logic or representation; exactitude does not enter into it. Far from being the sort of beautiful or precious objects that adorned the bourgeois interiors of the day, the objects of Cubism are very ordinary: tables, pitchers, bottles, glasses, fruit dishes and fruit, cigarette packets and pipes, musical instruments, newspapers... all of them common objects, of no value and in the end more timeless than all of the plasters, busts, and bouquets of academic art. Who was it who said that guitars and cigarette packets were the madonnas of the Cubists? By and large, they lived in a more urban world than that of the Impressionists or the Fauves, who found their inspiration in the countryside, or at least the suburbs. The Cubists tended to haunt Montmartre and the Latin Quarter rather than Giverny or Auvers-sur-Oise; from 1908 on, in any case, even when Braque and Picasso were in Céret or Sorgues, they painted just as they did in their studios in Paris.

More and more visitors began to appear in Braque's and Picasso's studios. And it was not only the poets who appreciated their art, for the 1908 exhibition at Kahnweiler's gallery had aroused a more general interest. Whether by coincidence or because the two artists' ideas were so much discussed, other painters soon showed signs of having adopted Cubism. The first were Fernand Léger and Robert Delaunay, in 1909; and then, in 1911, Juan Gris openly declared his indebtedness to Picasso and Braque. Other painters were not slow to follow the movement, for by then it had really become a movement: there was much talk of Cubism, a great deal of earnest discussion among such theorists as Metzinger and the Duchamp-Villon brothers. At the 1911 Salon des Indépendants a new generation of Cubists made a resounding first appearance: Léger, Delaunay, Metzinger, Gleizes, La Fresnaye, Lhote.... Neither Braque nor Picasso, knowing that they were well in advance of this still nascent movement, showed anything at this salon. In fact, they never took part in any of the group's public manifestations, irritated as they were by all the theories and codifications worked out by Metzinger and Gleizes, and even by Apollinaire. Disregarding all of the aesthetic or psychological reasons advanced in explanation of Cubism, laughing at the pseudoscientific verbiage and the fourth dimension that people tried to see in it, Braque and Picasso went on with their work. It mattered little to them that others had borrowed their idea of breaking the picture down by planes or that of the stenciled letters. Those were techniques they did not claim as their own. In any case, they were to discover plenty of others.

In 1911-1912, though Braque's pictures were still hermetic and only "readable" thanks to a few sparingly distributed signs or some inscriptions, Braque did endeavor to vary his approach. The *"Waltz" Still Life* surprises the viewer with a sort of grid of lines cutting across each other at right angles, rather like those of Mondrian some years later, the sharpness of the angles being reinforced by the picture's oval form and the scaffolding effect underlined by the appearance of imitation wood given to some of the rectangles. Above, but not entirely so, for the transparency distorts what would be an overly simple arrangement, there is a slantwise juxtaposition of a clarinet, a guitar, and a glass—or, rather, some elements which allow us to divine the presence of those objects. A touch of humor is introduced by an inscription that is distorted so that it can be read in spite of the clarinet partially covering it: *Valse*, a score for a dance band, doubtless for some important ball. The Cubists preferred popular dances or cafés-concerts to the elegant cotillions of the bourgeoisie—although Braque, who played the violin quite as well as the concertina, always paid homage to such composers as Bach or Mozart, as we may see in *Violin and Poster*, for instance. But I will come back to that later.

In contrast to the right-angled structures, other pictures are based on diagonals; an example is the *Still Life with Cluster of Grapes*, painted in 1912 at Sorgues, where Braque was spending the summer with Picasso, as we can tell from a fragment of inscription. In the tondo entitled *Soda* the diagonals intersect so much that they suggest a certain confusion, as though the work were seeking to express the effervescence of the drink that gives it its title. Except for the horizontality of the inscription "*Soda*," this perfectly circular work is visible from different angles; it could be hung 30 or 45 degrees out of the perpendicular and could even be turned round on its central axis—a peculiarity that may have been recalled by the painter Auguste Herbin, one of Picasso's neighbors at the Bateau-Lavoir, in a tondo he painted in 1917.

Quite apart from the construction of his pictures, Braque was equally careful to diversify their textures whenever they were in danger of settling into over-facile monochrome effects. In *Still Life with Cluster of Grapes* there are patches of grainy textured surface here and there, where the light sticks, as it were, for in these places the painter has mixed sand with his paint. This is also true of the *Fruit Dish* painted around the same time. Since that time, of course, Fontana, Tàpies, and many other painters have so pulverized color that this no longer astonishes anybody; but in 1912 it seemed like madness. "I introduced sand, sawdust, iron filings in my pictures.... I saw how much the color depended on the material. Take an example: if you soak two cloths, both white but of different materials, in the same dye, their colors will be different. It is obvious that this dependence that binds the color to the material is even more appreciable in paint. And what I particularly liked was that very *materiality* I had come up with thanks to the different materials I introduced in my pictures. For me, in short, it was a way of being further and further away from idealistic painting and increasingly close to the representation of things that I was looking for" (Interview with Dora Vallier). This diversification of the color is inevitably linked with Braque's research on brushwork, with which he especially concerned himself after his Fauvist period. Take, for instance, a particularly abstract picture painted in 1911, *The Violin*. The color here is not always spread out, but rather applied in little pointillist strokes. The painter was not trying to use this pointillism to break down the color, as in the case of Seurat and his school, but to change the texture of the color and give it a certain vibration. No less remarkable here is the way in which the color is dissociated from the forms. Since the painter is no longer trying to use the interplay of shades and penumbras within a perspective to create an illusion of depth in his picture, drawing and color can finally be completely separated—an antinomy that was to be regulated by the papiers collés and, later, by what came to be called synthetic Cubism. One might hazard a half-serious interpretation, not exclusive of the preceding one: is the violin—for we can recognize one here by some signs—intentionally blended into the harmony of the colors in the picture?

MUSIC AND MUSICIANS

Music figures very largely in Braque's work, and it was the painter's intention that this should be so. It may be worth our while to digress momentarily from our main purpose and consider all the ways in which it appears in his painting. Musical instruments are innumerable in the work of the Cubists and particularly so in that of Braque, Picasso, and Juan Gris. The most frequent are the guitar and the violin, but there are also, more particularly with Braque, the clarinet, the flute, the mandolin, and the piano; and we also find in his work some instruments rarely featured in painting, such as the zither, the mandola (a sort of lute) and the *bandonéon*, which is a kind of cross between a concertina and an accordion. Musical scores, for waltzes, *javas* (a popular rhythm of the day), and polkas are quite common in Braque's canvases. The studies of human figures, then, must have included quite a number of musicians, mostly guitarists and violinists. On the subject of these instruments, which are omnipresent in his work from 1909 on, Braque willingly explained: "Their modelling and volume belonged to the world of still life as I understood it. I was moving towards tactile space—or "manual" space, as I prefer to call it—and a musical instrument as an object had the peculiarity that

Still Life with Score for Duet. 1913. Oil on canvas, 92 × 65 cm. Museum of Modern Art, New York.

one could animate it by touching it. That is why I was so strongly attracted by musical instruments" (Interview with Dora Vallier). One can conceive this as regards the musical instruments, but what are we to say about the musical scores and staves so often featured on Braque's canvases? It is surprising that he never, at least as far as we know, used real scores in his papiers collés (as Picasso did, for instance, when he included a sonnet from the *Amours de Marie* set to music in *Music Sheet and Guitar* and in *Guitar and Wineglass*). I should also mention the written references to musical works or musicians that appear in his pictures from 1911 on, particularly in the papiers collés done between 1912 and 1914. There are references to Mozart and, of course, Bach, for whom Braque felt a particular devotion—in fact, there is a 1913 collage entitled *Bach Aria*. The works explicitly referred to in the canvases are called *Study, Solo, Sonata*: carefully constructed, introspective works that are quite expressive of Braque's temperament. We see the recurrence of such terms as *duo*, or even *duo pour flûtes*, in an *Oval Still Life: the Violin*, or in *Glass, Bottle and Pipe on a Table,* both painted in 1914. But was Braque not conducting at that time an interesting "duo" with Picasso? In the last of the canvases mentioned, curiously enough, we find the *duo pour flûtes* along with the letters *BAL*. The two kinds of music were so far from incompatible in the spirit of the Cubists, and of Braque more than any, that in a 1914 collage we find the words *Bal* and *Bach*, a propinquity that practically amounts to a manifesto.

As regards this question of music, one might be justified in advancing biographical reasons. As an adolescent in Le Havre, Braque had taken flute lessons from one of Raoul Dufy's brothers. He also played both the violin and the "shoulder-strap piano" (a term used to designate the accordion and similar instruments) well enough to enliven the gatherings of friends at the Bateau-Lavoir, where music always took pride of place. The old Douanier Rousseau used to play the violin when he visited them; Max Jacob was a pianist, a singer, and a composer when the spirit moved him; and I might also mention the guitarist Soler Cassabon, an inseparable friend of Reverdy and Juan Gris. This was a general phenomenon in Cubist circles; music was as important for the Duchamp-Villon brothers and their friends as it was for their neighbor Kupka and for Survage; Léger, Delaunay, Cendrars, and Milhaud were all assiduous frequenters of popular dance halls.... Thus the combination of *Violin and Palette* in one of Braque's still lifes is full of significance.

It should also be borne in mind that the painters and composers of the period felt very close to each other, probably because the problems of form confronting them at the time were not so very dissimilar. The painters felt constricted in the corset of traditional perspective, as did the musicians in that of traditionally tonality; and that was why, ever more radically from the early 1900s works of Schoenberg and Stravinsky, composers were to go beyond polytonality and end up practicing atonality. And if, as Milhaud said in 1923, "polytonality consists in different diatonic melodic lines in several keys at once, while atonality consists in melodic lines that do not belong to different keys," might we not compare polytonality to the multiple perspective known as "analytical," and atonality to that absence of perspective that we find in the later development called "synthetic" Cubism? However that may be, Darius Milhaud's First String Quartet (1912) was dedicated to the memory of Cézanne; Erik Satie and the Group of Six never missed their painter friends' *vernissages*; Igor Stravinsky, Florent Schmitt, and Edgar Varèse were on intimate terms with Picasso, Braque, Gleizes. ... Painters and musicians inevitably felt a desire to collaborate; and after World War I they were to be provided with abundant opportunities by the Russian and Swedish ballet companies. Let us anticipate in order to go a little further into this question: Braque was later to do the décors and costumes for various ballets, notably in 1924 for *Les fâcheux* by Georges Auric (with Diaghilev's Russian ballet company) and Milhaud's *Salade* (with the Comte de Beaumont's ballet company). And even though they did little work together, Braque and Satie were always very close—brought together by their common friendship with Picasso, a shared enthusiasm for the world of ancient Greece, and temperaments that, although fundamentally classical, did not reject either humor or the most daring novelties of form. Indeed, the first book illustrated by Braque was Satie's comedy *Le piège de Méduse*, for which he did three colored woodcuts in 1921; and in the same year he also painted a *Still Life with a Score by Satie*, an act of homage to the composer of *Parade* and *Socrate*.

Frequent association with musicians and an interest in the form of instruments were important factors. But we must go further if we wish to gain a deeper understanding of this affinity between Braque and music, the most abstract of all the arts. And I should point out that Braque always considered painting and music to be two quite different arts, with different media, which could not be merged without risking regrettable confusion; unlike Kandinsky or Kupka, he never gave his canvases titles like *Fugue* or *Nocturne* . He was quite ready, however, to explain his theories in terms of tonality or harmony: "You put a splash of yellow here and another at the other end of the canvas, and at once a relationship is established between them. The color acts like music, if you like to put it that way" (Interview with Dora Vallier). A change in tone is effected in painting in the same way as in music;

Braque's modification of the effect of one and the same color by the addition of sand, sawdust, or paper corresponds to the composer's use of different instruments to produce one and the same note. Since the Symbolists we have known that all sounds, forms, and colors have their *correspondences*. The Cubist planes that clash, intersect, and overlap have their counterparts not only in the breaches of syntax and logic practised by writers but also in the clashes, interruptions, and overlappings of music: in Stravinsky's *Petrushka*, for instance, the tune of *Elle avait une jamb' de bois* clashes with Lanner's *Waltz*, struggles against it and is then juxtaposed with it; and in Charles Ives' symphony *Holidays*, several marches and songs are played simultaneously, emerging here and there from the ensemble of notes.... Now surely this has just as much right to be called a collage as a piece of newsprint or oilcloth stuck on a canvas?

Braque probably also saw in music at once a *game* and a *construction*, with rules that can be infringed or not, music as *hazard* and *order*: calculation frustrating chance or in its turn playing its game of chance (a view evidently related to those games of chance and calculation that he loved to represent throughout his career: playing cards, dice, billiard tables, checkerboards). Who can tell whether it was not by conscious or unconscious analogy with the freedom the composer leaves to his interpreter that Braque painted a tondo like *Soda*, which can be hung at different angles? While other canvases are usually hung in a fixed, standard way, this one is variable in its perpendicularity; if necessary, as we have seen, it could even be hung from a revolving picture rail. Such analogies and correspondences are inevitable when we are dealing with an artist so very much committed to the spirit of his age, a spirit of which he is one of the principal interpreters. A contemporary of Braque, the American poet Wallace Stevens, wrote: "Joyce's language can be compared to the demolitions of Braque and Picasso or the music of the Austrians. ... When Braque says that the senses deform,

Construction on Paper. 1914. Sculpture on paper and cardboard. (Photo Archives Laurens.)

the spirit forms, he is speaking to the poet, the painter, the musician, and the sculptor" (*The Necessary Angel*).

PAPIERS COLLÉS

By 1912, Braque and Picasso so thoroughly embodied the spirit of the age in painting that they had inspired imitators who were beginning to be talked about—the last to join the movement being often the noisiest. Quite unconcerned, the two friends went off together as usual to spend their holidays at Sorgues. In their plastic language they had now reached such a point of convergence that their respective pictures were more similar than ever: the same strict drawing without any concession to the anecdotal, the same coloring of ochre tones, the same austere impersonality. If they did not want to get stuck in a single style, they had to move on. And the year 1912 was to see several major innovations. It was in May of that year, apparently, that it occurred to Picasso to stick on to one of his canvases a piece of oilcloth printed with a canework pattern; this *Still Life with Cane Chair* was the first example of collage (the inclusion of an object, or a fragment of an object, from outside), an idea that twentieth-century art was to exploit incessantly. Nor was Braque to be outdone: we have seen how he introduced techniques no less alien to the fine arts, like stencils and the "comb" used for producing imitation marble or wood. As to the inclusions of sand already mentioned, even those who pay most attention to meticulous chronology are uncertain: having first placed *Still Life with Cluster of Grapes* and *Fruit Dish* after the first papier collé (*Fruit Dish and Glass*), Pierre Daix later proposed to make them antedate it; neither solution, of course, is irrelevant, considering the closeness of the themes and, above all, of the concern with texture displayed in the canvases, *as though to make up for the color*: the inclusion of sand, flat surfaces of imitation wood that one would think to have been cut out. ... At the same time Braque also began to take an interest in sculpture and did several pieces in cardboard and paper, none of which, unfortunately, have survived; Picasso, more farsighted, preferred to make sculptures in materials that, although deliberately modest, were more durable—perhaps because he was the more "sculptural" of the two. "I was searching," Braque was later to recall. "I was doing sculpture in paper, and when Picasso wrote to me he used to address me as 'My dear old Wilbur.' On account of the aviator Wilbur Wright. For that work reminded him of aeroplanes. Then I brought sculpture into my canvases. Those were my first papiers collés, and with them color all at once returned to me" (Jean Paulhan, *Braque, le patron*). Whether before or after the papiers collés, all this research was their immediate contemporary.

Braque was to say that he had dreamed up his papiers collés by "a sort of revelation"; that may well be so, but a great deal of work had gone into paving the way. Having bought a roll of wallpaper imitating wood, of the sort used by decorators for covering panels and skirting boards, he cut out three pieces of it and stuck them onto the surface of a drawing entitled *Fruit Dish and Glass*; other papiers collés (for that was the name given to this technique to differentiate it from collage proper) were to follow. The first of these, such as *The Guitar*, were very simply arranged: on a drawing representing different planes, from which there emerge the outline of a guitar and the beginning of an inscription suggesting a newspaper, Braque placed a piece of striated imitation wood on which the drawing was prolonged slightly. This piece of *trompe-l'œil* wallpaper neither imitates nor follows the outline of the guitar; at most it suggests that the guitar is in wood of the same color; but its splash of color catches the eye all the more strikingly because it is placed in an uncolored drawing to which it is almost entirely unrelated—a separation of color from drawing much more radical than anything Braque had hitherto attempted in this line. In it we perceive the differences of material in an almost tangible way. Braque realized at once that with a humble material he had resolved an important problem: "The question of color was settled by the arrival of the papiers collés; that is something that the critics have never properly appreciated. It was then that I succeeded in distinctly dissociating color from form and seeing its independence in respect of form, for that was the great business: the color acts simultaneously with the form, but has nothing to do with it" (Interview with Dora Vallier). In order to diversify the effects, other sorts of papers very soon came to be stuck on to the base of paper, cardboard, or canvas: wallpaper, newsprint, tickets, labels, etc.

Papier collé, then, gave material expression to the dissociation of form and color; but it had plenty of other advantages. First of all, there was a historical *raison d'être*: "In the papiers collés," wrote Francis Ponge, "one should really see something other than a *material*. One should see a criticism of painting. And one should see what best corresponds, in the superintoxicated artist and art lover, to a distaste (which may arise) for painting—and the need to give the picture the support of something indisputable" (*Le peintre à l'étude*). Except for Picasso and Gris, who immediately realized the importance of the discovery, the papiers collés at first aroused anger and mockery. Cubism had already discarded the great traditional subjects of painting in order to seek greatness just as well in a simple fruit, a bird, or a chair; but now it was striking a blow against the sacrosanct profession and scoffing at the noble materials reserved to art (oil, grand papers, marble, bronze) by making use of "prefabricated" stuff and the most ordinary, everyday materials. The painter defended this choice openly: "To start out from ashes, from all that is lowest and most useless, and to bring it to light and life.... If one wants to have any chance of rising, one must know how to start out from below" (recorded by Stanislas Fumet in *Georges Braque*, 1965). In the painter's hands the simplicity of a piece of paper was to be transcended; like the stenciled letters before it, the imitation-wood wallpaper insistently reminds the viewer that what he sees before him is an object of art (of an artist and an artisan), a construction of the spirit. Some other writers have expressed this better. Louis Aragon: "The greatness of Cubism at this stage was that: absolutely anything, without even worrying about whether it was perishable or not, was used by these painters to express themselves; and so much the better if it was something quite valueless, something that even aroused disgust in their world" (*La peinture au défi*, 1930). Tristan Tzara: "In the evolution of painting the papiers collés mark in so many different aspects the most poetical and revolutionary moment, the touching expansion towards more viable hypotheses, a greater intimacy with everyday truths, the invincible affirmation of the provisional and of temporal, perishable materials, the sovereignty of thought" (*Cahiers d'art*, 2, 1931). One could imagine, even at that time, that the worthlessness of the material might be remedied by the painter through his art, but the perishable nature of such works was a formidable obstacle to their commercialization: one might expect to preserve the papiers collés reasonably well, but what future could there be for Braque's sculptures in paper? He said one day: "I do not believe in the eternal, the perpetual. The eternal is death; life is renewal" (*Ces peintres vous parlent*). And it is true that, while most of his papiers collés have been successfully preserved so far, despite some loss of color and the inevitable yellowing of the newsprint, none of his sculptures in paper have come down to us. We may regret this, but we cannot say that Braque did not stick to the principles he had formulated for himself. His problem as a painter was creation, not preservation.

During the time when Braque was composing his papiers collés the use he made of them was gradually diversified into a more and more complex language. *The Guitar* contains nothing but a drawing and a piece of the imitation-wood wallpaper. *Bach Aria*, executed only a few months later, contains two sorts of paper: two trapezoids of black paper stuck on to the drawing are themselves overlapped by a trapezoid of imitation-wood paper. Since the drawing is continued only on the pieces of black paper, the imitation-wood paper, despite its lack of thickness, really gives the impression that it is on top of them, as if the work existed in a space paradoxically lacking in thickness; and the whole ensemble makes up a sober construction corresponding to the sobriety of Bach's music. Within an oval painted on its rectangle of paper, *The Statue of Horror* creates a structure that includes four types of paper, among them a cinema program with clearly legible headlines—the title of the horror film programmed having doubtless appealed to the painter because of its naiveté and the ironical comment it would not fail to attract to his work. The oval surface of which Braque was always so fond is incomplete in *Violin and Pipe (The Daily Paper)*, but perhaps it is simply the form of a table seen from above (like the *Large Nude*) on which the objects would be laid flat. Each of these objects is provided with its own paper: imitation wood to *signify* the table itself, a piece of wallpaper edging for the tablecloth, black paper for the violin, the sound hole of which is traced in white, two pieces of newspapers that do not signify but *are* newspapers, and another piece of newsprint, not geometrical but cut out and shaded in the form of a pipe—and representing, naturally enough, a pipe. With much less elaborate means Braque created, in one and the same oval, an interesting composition in *The Ace of Hearts*: the oval is applied on, though at the same time seeming to be suspended over, the brown background that appears in the supposed hollowing out of the central motif. It is a heart really cut out of newsprint, however, that we find at the center of *The Post*, surrounded by cut-outs of wallpaper, torn (rather than regularly cut) imitation—wood paper, newsprint, and a piece of gray wrapping paper for tobacco. In *Still Life on a Table* we also have pieces of paper of different origins, but, apart from the fact that one of them was folded before being stuck on, the composition is enlivened with gouache: and thus we see how painting finally joins up with drawing and papiers collés, by tracing planes in imitation papier collé!

With *The Portuguese* (1911), words and inscriptions first appeared in the canvases of the Cubists, whether for aesthetic reasons (the form of the letters and playing with the depth of the work), to render explicit homage (to Bach, to Mozart), or even because lettering and inscriptions are so much a part of modern life that they must always be taken into account. Apollinaire wrote: "Picasso and Braque introduced sign lettering and other inscriptions in their works of art because in any modern town inscriptions, signs and publicity play a very important artistic role and are suitable for this purpose" (*Der Sturm*, February 1913). Not only Braque and Picasso took this fact into account; in fact almost all of the Cubists did. Besides, even when these isolated fragments were used for realistic effects, simply as pieces of posters, tickets, newspaper headlines, or titles of scores, they tended to acquire a poetical power that had to do with literature rather than painting. *Concert, Bal, L'écho d'Athènes, Valse, Rasoir Gillette*: all of these fragments, isolated from their habitual context, are imbued with a disquieting force, which the painters were not at all shy of using. With the appearance of the papiers collés such inscriptions multiplied, all the more when newsprint and printed matter were used: in these cases the color of the paper was hardly more important than the legible words that might appear on it. The way in which certain words and phrases stood out when the paper was cut was not always entirely artless.

As we know, life with the "Picasso gang" was anything but boring. With or without the assistance of humorously inclined friends like Apollinaire, Max Jacob, or Reverdy, Picasso and Juan Gris have left in their plastic works quite a few esoteric or rather "broad" puns that we can still appreciate. Since Braque has always been regarded in retrospect as the most serious-minded of the group, it has only recently been discovered that humorous touches and puns are not so rare in his work. Some of them are evident: we smile readily at *The Statue of Horror* and we may have observed in *The Post* that the newspaper headline, truncated and partly hidden by the gray tobacco wrapping, reads "Le Cœur" (The Heart), while underneath we may also read "organe de madame" (lady's organ) and a cutout heart shape. More discreet, perhaps because they involve rather too ribald a double meaning, are other touches that do not leap to the eye so quickly; in a gouache with collage, which is in the Kunstmuseum of Ulm, for instance, along a strip of corrugated cardboard we see a fragment of newsprint cut out in such a way that we can read the sequence of headlines: "Maladies des deux" (Diseases of couples), "Impuissance" (Impotence), and then "Hygiène du mariage" (Marital hygiene).... It might perhaps be advisable not to exaggerate the supposed esotericism of these punts; it is surely a little excessive, from ignorance of the pronunciation of the word *broc* (pitcher) or of what a *pyrogène* (pyrogen) once meant, to see a self-portrait in a picture in which Braque has depicted a pitcher, and in a pyrogen an instrument for lighting an oil stove; or to consider the inscription "SONATE," altered to "SO-ATE" by a fold in the paper, to be something which is pronounced *souhait* and therefore means *desire* (Alvin Martin, *Braque: Papiers collés*, Paris, 1982). I imagine that Braque and his friends would have laughed heartily if they had known that the University would come up with such interpretations of their intentions.

During the years 1912 to 1914, when they were creating their papiers collés most intensively, neither Braque nor Picasso neglected painting; their painting, however, was to be noticeably affected by the new technique. *Still Life with Glass and Newspaper* (1913) largely retains the fundamentally ochre tones of earlier paintings, but its structure is quite different. It is now, despite some signs indicating the presence of vague objects, a superimposition of rectangles without any thickness which do not intersect but partially overlap, like a bundle of papers that has come undone; these rectangles are, in fact, sheets of paper from newspapers or musical scores, and some are cut as in a papier collé; but others, which are parts of furniture, or of moldings, are no less flat. In *The Musician's Table* (1913), a hesitantly oval composition, the analogy with the papiers collés is more marked, because the objects that are not flat have practically disappeared; the planes have a certain transparency, as if they were made of tracing paper, but thanks to the presence of certain contrasting forms in black and white they have much more presence, an almost tactile intensity. And if we now turn to an oval canvas also painted in 1913, *Glass, Violin and Music*

Paper, we may well think that in this *trompe-l'œil* imitation of what is already imitation the painter is amusing himself with a parody of papiers collés: playing with a drawing that is carefully done but only barely shaded with color, three bands or strips stand out, two yellow and one brown, as though in an attempt to be mistaken for cut-out paper, an attempt in which we even see an effect of torn paper at the botton of the perpendicular paper. Thus with the aid of the papiers collés we come to what the critics came to call synthetic Cubism (though this concept as worked out by Juan Gris has more to do with painting and that painter's methods). The painter no longer analyzes his subject with a view to breaking it up in various planes on his canvas. Indeed, he no longer starts out from the object but rather from the canvas itself, and the overall effect suggests that he has arranged planes of color on that canvas and then added, as though incidentally, some traces of the real in this abstract space: rectangles that are the sheets of a waltz score (the inclusion of the word *valse* anchors us to a certain reality), shaded curves that make a glass, and an undulating oblong form that without the sound-holes would be a guitar rather than a violin.

The most evident effect produced by the papiers collés on Braque's painting was that of reintroducing color by transposing one technique into another. The imitation sheets of papier collé in such a picture as *Glass, Violin and Music Paper* are plain to be seen. Later on, Braque decided to diversify the effects. A painting like the 1914 *Glass, Bottle and Pipe on a Table* (a standard theme for still lifes) can be presented as a synthesis of the Cubist experiences. The table is seen from above and forms a rectangle that expands into other rectangles (as in the works of the Italian Futurists by the effect of the light), unless the sheets of paper stick out beyond it; and it is also seen "full-face," as is indicated by the drawer; and slantwise, as we see in a triangle painted to represent imitation-wood wallpaper. The objects are seen flat, but without any regard to scale and in a great variety of presentation: as though it were the object closest to us, the sharp-edged glass seems to have been cut out and transferred onto the canvas; the pipe, the bottle, and the playing card interpenetrate, not by transparency but because they are placed in a multidimensional space; the printed objects (the advertisement for a dance, a music score, and an indeterminate rectangular form) lead lives of their own, receding from the table and invading the surrounding space.... The work uses tangible references to reality, but inserts them in a world of colors and forms in which there is no longer any place for everyday logic. Thanks to multiple effects of transparence or thickness in the planes, of colors in flat surfaces, in layers of imitation wood or in an infinite iridescence of little dots, the whole work is imbued with an intensely vibrant life. Whether it is analytical or synthetic hardly matters; for here Cubism attains a perfection that goes beyond all denominations and labels. During the summer of 1914, however, something that had nothing to do with art was to disrupt Braque's whole life and work: World War I.

WAR

Braque was working at Sorgues when mobilization was announced. In Paris, Picasso saw Braque and Derain off on the train that was to take them to the front. Picasso himself would stay and continue to paint; his two friends were to undergo a terrible experience that would not leave them unchanged. Less than a year later Braque was seriously wounded in the head; on coming out of the

Woman with Mandolin. 1917. Oil on canvas, 92×65 cm. Musée d'Art Moderne du Nord, Villeneuve d'Asq.

ensuing coma, he underwent trepanation and, after a period of blindness, began a long convalescence. He was more fortunate than his friends Apollinaire and Duchamp-Villon, however: he survived. Early in 1917 a banquet was held in Paris to celebrate his recovery. He started painting again the following summer, but the war had nonetheless meant three years of complete interruption of his work. Though taking into account all that had been done during those three years by his friends—Picasso, with whom he was no longer on quite such close terms, and more particularly Gris and Laurens—he was to take up his work again at the point where he had left it before the war.

Rather than hesitancy, properly speaking, it was a change of direction that appeared in his new works, painted during 1917 and 1918, when he was trying different experiments. We can see this by comparing *The Man with the Guitar* (1914) with two later works on a similar theme, the 1917 *Woman with Mandolin* and *The Musician*, painted in 1917-18. While the prewar canvas is a mass of quivering planes, *Woman with Mandolin* is static, arranged in accordance with three rather *intentional* perpendiculars, as were the trees in the 1917 *View of L'Estaque from the Hotel Mistral*. The angular forms contrast with the underlined curves of the face, the hands, and the instrument; one is reminded of Juan Gris in the plastic pun that turns the outline of the bust and the head framed in black strokes into a guitar shape. An even greater impression of impassiveness is produced by *The Musician*, which is more affected by Picasso's research at the time than by that of Gris: despite the textures of imitation wood or imitation cloth, there is no real interplay between the different planes; the bust and the face form a single plane divided into geometrical surfaces, though the contrast with the lower part of the body, of the dress in which there is a certain depth, produces a strange effect on anybody viewing it: it is a beautiful work, but the character has a somewhat ghostly air, far removed from the sensuous world of the musicians Braque painted before the war.

The hardening of the angles to be observed in *The Musician* is still more evident in a series of paintings that Braque did almost simultaneously. The geometrical purism that characterizes them was exceptional in his work, but one can see that this was a path on which he might have gone further. After having done some experiments with diamond shapes, he returned to a figure with which he felt at home, the oval form. But since he was working with rulers at that time, the figure became an oblong octagon with regular angles and with the colors applied in eight regularly traced internal triangles (Picasso, in 1918, had placed a still life in a hexagon). This octagon is contained in the rectangle of the picture, following its diagonals and medians, and in the spider's web of this structure are caught three objects treated in a Cubist manner now familiar: a tumbler, a packet of tobacco, and two molded bands, which are perhaps two sides of a frame. In this, too, the work is strange: the three objects, caught like flies in the center of this cobweb rather than posed on a pedestal table, are incongruous in their geometrical surroundings; they stand out from it as though they were part of a papier collé effect: the tumbler has the air of something cut out and glued to the longest median, and the two moldings could easily be printed imitation wood. At the same time, in fact, Braque also did a large papier collé in which the paper motifs, painted by hand, were cut out and stuck onto the center of a similar spider's web.

In order to take up his work again where he had left it at the beginning of the war, Braque went back to his papiers collés. Although he had hardly used this technique at all since 1915, other artists had taken it up on their own account; his friend Laurens used it for a long time to come, and with very felicitous inventiveness. Braque himself created a final masterpiece using this technique, *Guitar and Clarinet* (Museum of Art, Philadelphia). To represent two musical instruments on a table he used a complex structure in which papers of various types overlap. Contrary to his prewar custom, drawing plays hardly any part in this work—not even for the shadows, which are here represented by shaded paper. The drawn holes in the guitar and the clarinet, or the fragments of a stave, serve as touches of irony rather than as real elements of drawing. The drawing is replaced by the streakings of the different pieces of imitation wood orientated in different directions according to the angle at which the paper is stuck on. An evident, and delectable, effect of relief is provided by the clarinet in corrugated cardboard; the casualness with which Braque liked to treat—or ill-treat—his clarinets is always particularly entertaining for the viewer.

In spite of such successes, Braque pursued the path of the papiers collés through only very rare exceptions and those in a rather different spirit than before (the 1919 *Still Life at Galanis* is a painted piece stuck onto paper, which produces the effect of a fragment of pottery, although the 1961 *Bird in the Foliage* is closer to the earlier works insofar as it presents a plain form stuck onto a background of newspapers cut up and colored with some splashes of gouache). Doubtless he had the impression that he would be repeating himself and that that would risk returning to the process. After all, it was he himself who said: "Ideas, like clothes, wear out and are distorted by use." Besides, there were plenty of techniques that he had as yet only partially explored: sculpture and engraving, for instance, both of which he was to go in for quite a bit in later years. But undoubtedly Francis Ponge has best explained the reasons for Braque's abandonment of

papiers collés and his necessary return to painting in its traditional techniques: "He had to go beyond that because, once conceived, it was too easy, not worth continuing—too easy a trick, in short. And he had to replace that indisputable-irrepressible-element by something else, something more aleatory, more heroic, although at first glance less revolutionary: by confining himself to painting in oils, the art of the bad old academic painters" (*Le peintre à l'étude*).

It was indeed through painting in oils that Braque was to regain all his authority, in the course of the last year of World War I. He embarked upon several series of still lifes, one of which centers on a clarinet, with or without other instruments. *Clarinet and Music Album* (1918) surprises us with a facility not found in such rather coldly calculated works as *The Musician* and the geometrical pictures. This picture descends from synthetic Cubism, recapturing very well the interplay of clean planes that characterized that style of painting, although without any attempt to make them reminiscent of the papiers collés; the colors follow the drawn forms, the brushwork is rapid, the stippling disposed of without excessive precision— quite the opposite, in short, of the *trompe-l'œil* effects in *The Musician*. One can no longer guess what these planes are supposed to represent (a table or a tablecloth?), but they form a dynamic background for the only two objects schematically depicted in the center of the picture: a clarinet and a music album that are enough to flabbergast any lover of good sense or good taste. For the painter has drawn them, not only in defiance of all rules of perspective but as though he had no more than a vague idea of their appearance. He could hardly have expressed any better his contempt for the anecdotal aspect of things. The distorted rectangles of the pages only undulate slightly at the bottom, and the clarinet resembles a flat hammer or a T-square; a rounded instrument *par excellence*, here we see it reduced to irregular rectangles, without any thickness as far as its bell, which appears to be open only through a sort of orifice drawn in ostentatiously slapdash fashion. It may be just permissible for the instrument's reed to be represented by no more than an odd-looking mouthpiece and its keys replaced by some rather improbable holes; but to see its upper part passing through the music album, like a needle through a page? How better could he express that neither logic nor verisimilitude is the business of painting? This work is, first and foremost, a perfect balance of forms and colors; as for academic figuration, in this picture the painter makes fun of it with considerable wit.

THE TWENTIES

When peace returned to Europe, Cubism was by no means dead. It even received a new lease on life in 1916-17, not only because the artists had not abandoned it but also because it was supported by a first-class new review, Pierre Reverdy's *Nord-Sud* (1917-18), and because Léonce Rosenberg, a dynamic art dealer wedded to the cause of Cubism, had taken Kahnweiler's place when the latter was exiled during the war. To *Nord-Sud* Braque contributed illustrations and his very enlightening *Pensées sur la peinture*; these first brief notes were not to be collected and prepared for publication until thirty years later. In 1919, Rosenberg, who had become Braque's dealer, organized a one-man show of the artist's work. Picasso, Gris, and Laurens continued to practice synthetic Cubism and gradually brought it to a sort of classicism (Picasso's *The Three Musicians* was painted in 1921), and Léger and Delaunay were working with color and mingling abstract and figurative elements in their works. For some time Braque seemed to be participating in this belated form of Cubism, though always remaining independent (*Clarinet and Music Album*) and seeking a classicism of his own. But Picasso, even during his continuation of Cubism, was already working on a return to realistic drawing, followed by not a few of the former Cubists (La Fresnaye, Rivera, Herbin).... The purists and the innovators sought in vain to adapt certain advances made by Cubism to contemporary taste. During the twenties all of the former Cubists gradually turned to other genres—except Juan Gris, who was to develop a Cubism of his own. We shall see how Braque, too, drew away from Cubism without thereby turning towards realism or opting for abstraction.

Braque, however, could not fail to be irritated, both by the way Cubism had been fossilized by the followers and dogmatists of the movement and by the nihilism, the negation of all aesthetic values, that was flaunted by the Dadaists rampant in Paris between 1920 and 1923. Neither the cold calculation of the former nor the frenzied subjectivity of the latter held any appeal for him. In his notes published in *Nord-Sud* in 1917 he had written: "I love the rule that corrects emotion," but shortly afterwards he was to add: "I love the emotion that corrects the rule." For one of the constants in Braque's work is that willpower is always combined with emotion, self-control with passion. The early twenties, during which the painter did not produce much work, were to express, beyond the declaration of independence implicit in the 1918-19 clarinet series, a real reaction on his part.

The two *Canephorae* exhibited at the 1922 Salon d'automne caused considerable surprise, reassuring some viewers and disconcerting others. Then, as now, one either liked or did not like these life-size female figures bearing baskets of fruit; but at least one had to agree with André Salmon, an old friend from Cubist days who certainly did not much appreciate them, that they have "an extraordinary dignity." In Braque's work the bathers and nudes had disappeared some fifteen years earlier—after the 1907 *Large Nude*, which likewise marked a reorientation of his art. The *Canephorae* owe less to Ingres than do certain neo-classical female figures being painted at the time by Picasso (it is significant that in 1922 Braque should also have begun a study of a *Woman with Mandolin* after Corot). The *Canephorae* are figures quite as impersonal as the traditional female bearers of fruit of Greek antiquity by which they are inspired. They are never bacchantes, or even dancers, but always characters moving slowly or in repose; the faces are serene or inexpressive, the bodies are solidly—indeed, muscularly—constructed with large, firm strokes and with nothing of the pearly quality of bodies painted by Degas or Renoir, nothing of the sensuousness, historically closer, of the works of a painter like Pascin. Although monumental, they lack the deliberate roundness and heaviness of Picasso's fat women, or of the later sculptures of Laurens. But it is not perhaps quite by chance that, particularly in the graphic studies or gouaches (*Woman with Bicycle, Seated Bather*, etc.), one is reminded of the contemporary Greek painter Fassianos; we shall have to return later, moreover, to this question of Grecism in Braque's work. This new interest in the human figure, which was really an interest in curve and gesture rather than movement, led Braque to design the costumes and décor for the ballets *Les fâcheux, Salade*, and *Zéphyr et Flore* between 1923 and 1925. Whether with nudes, canephorae, or bathers, until 1927 Braque was to continue his exploration of this theme of dark, massive women that have been variously compared to those of Gauguin and Poussin. This inclusion in a tradition was to bring a sneer from Vlaminck, an old Fauvist painter

already on the decline and full of belligerence against the Cubists: "Since Cubism does not have the same lethal effects as syphilis, not all of its practitioners have died; and the survivors now claim the authority of Poussin, Corot and Ingres" (*Tournant dangereux*, 1929). This, of course, is mere caricature. Braque had no more broken with his past than Picasso. Apart from the fact that the *Canephorae* and the *Bathers* are not unrelated to his earlier work, the multiplicity of his interests could easily lead to his simultaneously expressing himself in two different languages: that of tradition in the deepest sense of the term and that of the avant-garde that had not forgotten Cubism. And there again we find, quite naturally, an attitude similar to Picasso's.

During the years from 1921 to 1927, when Braque was painting his canephorae and bathers, he also painted a series of still lifes with groups of objects on a mantelpiece. Thus we find—and will continue to find—the painter working in series (the series of the pedestal tables, the boats, the studios, the birds, etc.), which has caused some critics to say, wrongly, that his repertory of themes was limited. Many other painters were doing the same, Picasso most of all; but while Picasso tended to seize a subject and exhaust it through intense activity in the shortest possible lapse of time, Braque preferred to come back to his themes every now and then, with a varying number of variations, in the course of a process of reflection that might last several years. Such were the consistency and slowness of a progress that the painter himself was always careful to stress, and which should not be forgotten: "I have always respected the subject, for I consider it indispensable. I have chosen for myself the subjects of my pictures, as other painters have freely chosen theirs. In this, as in other things, one must know how to limit oneself, how to restrict oneself by choosing themes that are definitively closer to one's own nature.... If I do not paint from life, it is because I want to be more direct" (Interview with Tériade, 1928). Or again, referring to his way of working on several canvases at the same time, sometimes for years together: "Just think of the advantages of working without a model—the apples would be rotten long before I finished my canvas.... I find that one has to work slowly. Everyone who looks at the canvas goes back over the same road as the artist...." (Interview with Dora Vallier, 1954). Braque's works, unlike those of many other painters, do not always have an immediate effect on the viewer; one needs time to become familiar with them, to go beyond one's first impression—all the more so because they refuse to provide spectacular effects. What could be less sensational than a guitar and a fruit dish on a mantelpiece? The theme was as good as any other, and Braque certainly intended to show that it had enormous possibilities for anybody sufficiently alert. Beginning in 1921, then, he took six years to work out this theme completely. As an example we might take a *Mantelpiece* from the middle of this period (1923), the one in the Kunsthaus in Zürich; it is a work, moreover, with which Braque was so pleased that he repeated it with hardly any variations in a version now in the West Palm Beach Museum. This canvas is a truly astonishing synthesis of realistic detail (moldings and marble of the mantelpiece, form and color of the cluster of grapes), cut-out planes inherited from synthetic Cubism (the raised plane of the shelf of the mantelpiece and the objects, the truncated lower part of the mantelpiece, the cut-out of shade on the objects), and even the flat geometrical surfaces deriving from the papiers collés (fender, hearth, wall, moldings, and perhaps the looking-glass over the mantelpiece). In the course of his different versions, Braque was to make modifications in the choice and arrangement of the objects

The Sauceboat and the Asparagus. 1924. Oil on canvas, 21.5×32.5 cm. Galerie Maeght, Paris.

in this still life, but he always made use of the contrasting effect between their Cubist schematization and cutting on the one hand and, on the other, the details and almost traditional perspective of the back and front of the mantelpiece. There is even a crack in the marble, at the corner of the mantelpiece, which is reproduced in all the different versions. But there is no reason why this should be seen as a veristic detail. Anybody who has lived in a furnished room or apartment will be aware of the importance of a broken-off corner of marble. The emotive force of an object often comes from some little imperfection that personalizes it; like a scar on a human body, a break or crack shows that the object has lived. Even, and indeed especially, if they are painted from memory ("even if I do not paint from life," as Braque himself said), the objects live with man.

The Marble Table, a masterpiece painted in 1925, derives directly from the research that went into *The Mantelpiece*: the same perpendicular arrangement, the same contrast between abstract planes and clearly recognizable objects; though here, conversely, it is the objects in the still life itself rather than their surroundings that are seen in traditional perspective. *The Marble Table* is undoubtedly more impressive than *The Mantelpiece*, thanks to its more exquisite and less clear-cut color harmonies, and also because its composition, based on diagonals in green, is much more dynamic.

Apart from these large still lifes, so complex that they are almost studio landscapes, Braque did not neglect the simpler sort of still life that was from now on his most characteristic genre. *The Sauceboat and the Asparagus* is his response to Manet's *Asparagus*, the theme being further developed by adding the sauce to eat the vegetable with. *Fruit, Jug, Pipe* and *The Basket of Flowers*, also painted in 1924, are simple compositions in close-up with a sort of good-natured charm. These small-format paintings, casual-seeming and without any of the austerity of Cubism, are to Braque what "studies" are for a musician; it is clear that in them he pays particular attention to something he always considered fundamental: the brushwork. *Fruit, Jug, Pipe* is impastoed and surrounded with a thick stroke that contrasts with the lightly applied motifs of the wallpaper in the background or the grain of the wood. In *The Basket of Flowers* the touch gives the flowers a granular effect and deepens the contrast between the colors of the petals; the basket returns to rectangles applied in horizontal strokes, as in the painter's Fauvist days, and the table is treated with a "comb," evoking the parallel lines of the wood. The touch is so sensuous that one occasionally almost thinks one can grasp the objects depicted. Just look at the asparagus: one

could eat them! In his notes Braque wrote: "It is not enough to make what one paints visible, one must also make it touchable." At the same time he took the occasion to try his hand at unusual formats: octagonal pictures such as *Fruit, Jug, Pipe*, horizontally oblong pictures like *Fruit, Glass, Knife*, high, narrow pictures like the two *Still Lifes*, the one with the *pitcher* and the one with the *fruit dish* (1926-27). The format of the latter two was dictated by utilitarian and decorative considerations (they were intended to occupy two narrow spaces on the walls of a dining room), but we may see quite clearly that Braque did not confine himself to furnishing the space with them; he even added to his restrictions by placing his motifs, alternately Cubist or realistic, in curious oblong shapes and presented them, with a touch of humor, as though they were seen through keyholes. Works such as these led an observer of the day, Alejo Carpentier, to say: "The whole of modern art is a series of broadsides against the decorative style as an end in itself, which does not mean that occasionally, without such being his special intention, after accomplishing a higher plastic purpose, the modern painter may not produce admirable decorative effects. There is nothing more agreeable from the decorative point of view than a Cubist composition by Braque. In Braque, however, this decorativism is not a fault, for in his canvases there is *something else*" (*Chronique d'avril*, 1929).

At the end of the twenties, landscapes, which Braque had not painted since 1911, made a definitive reappearance in his work. They were mostly seaside scenes, coinciding with the painter's return to the Normandy of his childhood; in 1931 he was to have a house built at Varengeville, near Dieppe, where he was to spend part of the year from then on when he was not in Paris. Braque was not the sort of painter who sets up his easel and spends long hours working in the open air; he usually painted by taking his inspiration from (at most) such scenery as he saw and arranging it to suit himself. Just as he assembled guitars, glasses, and newspapers on a pedestal table for a still life, so he assembled boats, a stretch of cliff, or a hut, an intentionally rather theatrical décor that he was to remain fond of for the rest of his life. *The Three Boats*, painted in 1929, is a landscape—seen at night, one would say—very lightly rendered: a sea with dark, slack water, a clean-brushed sky, stippled pebbles, a hut cut across by a patch of shadow. The weft of the canvas shows through everywhere. The whole presents an impression of unreality, because the depth is indistinct: although the elements—sea, sky, cliff, and shore—do have a certain density, the hut has not the slightest thickness and the beached boats are foreshortened, as tubby as cockleshells, with enormous masts. The details of their boards seem engraved rather than painted; seen at once from above and from the side, they are as unrealistic as possible. And yet this work, paradoxically, emanates an impression of peace and calm.

THE THIRTIES

Braque had not given up the avant-garde research with which his name was associated. The year 1929 brought works of a type that was to be characteristic of the first half of the thirties, with a sense of casualness and humorous or aggressive distortions for which the model had in all likelihood been supplied by Picasso. *Fruit Dish and Napkin* (1929) divides the space into six perpendicular bands or strips that, like the folds of a curtain, distribute the shade over the motif and the background, both drawn in thick, cheerful strokes; the diamond shapes of the tablecloth suddenly turn up to form the background against which, with a profusion of curves and curls unusual in Braque, we see two pieces of fruit, a rolled table napkin and a fruit dish containing the inevitable bunch of grapes. Everything is painted with a joy of lines and color, a healthiness, that recalls Matisse as much as Picasso. Equally sinuous were the human figures Braque painted at the same time: the 1931 *Recumbent Nude with Pedestal Table* is an odalisque with webbed feet, a distorted bust in which a simple W forms the breasts, two frail, disproportionate arms, and a single, cyclopean eye. In this work, in which the painter thumbs his nose as it were at the odalisques of Ingres and Manet, a certain Surrealist influence is evident. *The Beach* (1931) and its grotesquely blown up characters, with their spindly limbs and their pinlike heads with three hairs floating in the breeze (an obvious wink at Picasso), are both drawn and painted barbarously: the hastily sketched lines, the colors quite unrelated to the forms, take us at one bound to the work produced by "crude art" and the Cobra group fifteen or twenty years later. In *The Bathers*, painted in the same year, with clumsy shapes like seaweed or the forms then being deployed by Arp, Miró, or Tanguy, the shade and the color follow the drawing even less, and the drawing itself is dislocated to such a point that at times the limbs are detached from the trunks. One may prefer other paintings to these works done by a grimacing Braque. This research, however, was to lead to very interesting repercussions in a quite different type of work that the painter took up at this time.

In 1931, thanks to a commission from Ambroise Vollard, Braque, who had not engraved anything for twenty years, undertook a series of engravings; it is significant that he should have chosen to illustrate Hesiod's *Theogony*. (In *Georges Braque: Nouvelles sculptures et plaques gravées*, published in 1960, Christian Zervos provides conclusive proof of Braque's ties with Greek antiquity, even apart from his declared interest in Hesiod and Pindar.) This series of engravings was ready in 1932. In the meantime, and afterwards, this work was to lead to a certain number of other, similar works. The little oil *Athena* is the exact equivalent, and in almost the same format, of one of the engravings in the *Theogony*. Although the works are far from the surrealizing expressionism of *The Beach* or *The Bathers*, their technical relationship is obvious: since the color and the drawing are independent, the sinuous lines of the latter are read under splashes of color that, following them only very vaguely, distort them even more and give them a real plastic dynamism and yet at the same time great coherence.

It was at this time, too, that Braque introduced a new working technique, which he was to call "incised plaques" and which partook of the nature of sculpture quite as much as of engraving or painting. Since the sculptures in paper done between 1912 and 1914, Braque had hardly done anything in this line but a little bronze in 1920. The first of these incised plaques that he did in the thirties had neither color nor relief. On a smooth plaster surface coated in black, the stroke of the stylus or the scratching produces a pure white. The sometimes dense but always elegant interlacings of this drawing in negative always represent the gods and heroes of Greek mythology: a nereid on her marine mount, Hercules shooting arrows at the birds of the Stymphalian lake, some scraped surfaces indicating the water. One is reminded of the stylization of pre-Hellenic figures or of certain ancient coins. Braque was to do several series of incised plaques in the course of his career; together with some sculptures of characters and animals that he embarked on at the very end of the thirties,

they represent an original and important aspect of his *œuvre*.

Around 1934 Braque returned to his earlier taste for vivid colors in a series of still lifes: *The Pink Tablecloth* (1933), *Red Still Life* (1934), *The Yellow Tablecloth* (1937).... In these works angular forms and rounded forms more or less granulated with sand mingle happily. The works are gay and strange for, although in certain signs one recognizes the familiar world of Braque's still lifes (fruit, glasses, pipes, music scores, baskets), in other forms, bizarre and one might almost say soft structures, one hesitates to point out a guitar or a white aubergine. This whimsical aspect plays no small part in the pleasure of anybody viewing these canvases.

From 1936 to 1939 Braque embarked on a series of works that took painting and music as their themes; the first of these is undoubtedly *Woman with Easel*, of which he painted two versions in the same year. The picture is arranged in three bands, in accordance with a method familiar to the painter: the first contains the easel, the picture on it and the palette; the second, lighter in tone, shows the woman seen full-face; the third, again darker, presents as though in a shadow show the other half of the woman's face, in an updated version of an old Cubist procedure. Everything about the character is calm and sedate; it is a long way from the cheerfully distorted bathers painted five years earlier. After a series of works in which the theme is enriched—among them the very beautiful 1937 *Duet*—in 1939 Braque painted *The Painter and His Model*, considered one of the most important canvases he ever did.

The Painter and His Model is a traditional theme in painting in which the artist places himself more or less directly on stage; it was in this way that Picasso used it. But Braque had always avoided direct autobiography, and even with a subject like this he remained conspicuously outside: apart from the fact that he had not used a model for many years, he in no way resembled the bald, bearded painter with a cigarette between his lips who appears in this picture. As in *Woman with Easel*, the characters are cut in two according to the shade by a light source that seems to be in the ceiling and illuminates the half of the space occupied by the painter more than that occupied by the model, the division being made on either side of the enormous easel that presides over the center of the canvas, and the difference of light appearing in the alteration of the coloring of the paper on the wall. Like the imitation-wood effect of the easel, its large and rather gaudy pattern of leaves reminds us of the period of the papiers collés. For all its simplicity and admirable construction of shade and color, this picture is nonetheless a little mysterious on account of certain details to which nobody has paid much attention and which cannot be due to chance; Braque would have left nothing to chance in such an important picture. Sitting squarely in his big armchair, is the painter not in the same position as his model? Certainly the model has the air of somebody standing, but in the drawing traced of her on the canvas she is clearly sitting. Besides, what is she holding in her left hand? Rather than some indeterminate instrument, might it not be a palette with paintbrushes? If so, her right hand would not be holding some draped cloth, but might have a paintbrush, or a stick of charcoal—like the painter's hand that we do not see. Thus painter and model would be alike, in a mirror image. Narcissism on the painter's part, or pointlessness of engaging a model if the painter has everything in himself? It is difficult to say. And another detail: the walls are bare with the exception of something behind the model and visible through the hangings, which may be either a picture representing only an abstract form

Studio with Black Vase. 1938. Oil on canvas, 97 × 130 cm.
Private collection, New York.

or a mirror: narcissism again, and all the more so since what is then reflected in it is not the model's hair but one of the uprights of the easel, in the form of a lyre. But what do we see on this imposing easel? A little painting in oils in which we can recognize distinctly a drawing of the model, realistic but discreet, and an assemblage of gaudily colored geometrical figures. Is Braque making a humorous allusion to the two types of painting that monopolized the public's attention at the end of the thirties—the return to the figurative (the Forces nouvelles group, for instance) and radical abstraction (the Abstraction-Création group)? Or else, since the age of the painter represented would exclude the idea of a retrospective look at the heroic days of Cubism, is he mocking those belated Cubists who "cubicized" from a model? One would naturally be wary of advancing an explanation with certainty; but however it may be, in this synthesis-picture that closes such a carefully meditated series one cannot fail to perceive Braque's irony beyond the seriousness of the subject.

The period certainly did not lend itself to broad comic effects, which in any case were not much to Braque's taste. The late thirties were anxious years: war in the Far East, war in Spain, the rise of the fascist régimes.... In the numerous works in which the painter represented the tools of his trade—easel, paintbrushes, palette—the colors grew somber or else the objects were distorted in a disquieting way. The *Still Life with Palette* painted in 1939 no longer has the forms and colors of the 1938 *Pedestal Table*, also presided over by the painter's instruments. The later canvas is one of harrowing expressionism: the forms are heavy, brutally constructed, and without any concession to beauty, for even the flowers in the vase have the same feeling; the palette is like a pair of gaping jaws, and it is easy to guess what the partly hidden white rectangle under it represents: *Le Journal*, with news from the world outside....

It was at this time that Braque began to paint a series under the general title of *Vanitas*—not so much because he wished to paint work in response to circumstances, but because he could not fail to be affected by the growing disquiet in the world around him and to ask himself the consequent questions. *Studio with Black Vase*, painted in 1938, assembles the familiar material of the studio, but quite close to the palette there is a rounded object with dents and carefully rendered shading: a skull. Its presence is intended to be a discreet reminder of the transitory, if not vain, character of art (palette, easel, canvases) and the world of the senses (flowers, fabrics). A premonitory theme, and one which the painter would not abandon for some time to come.

WAR AND POSTWAR

With 1939 came war again and, after some months, the debacle. In 1940, Georges and Marcelle Braque had to leave Normandy and Paris. It was all the more necessary since a travelling retrospective exhibition of the painter's works in the United States that year did not exactly win him much favor with the occupying forces. Braque took refuge first in the Limousin and then in the Pyrenees, but the end of 1940 found him back in Paris; there he was to stay throughout the Occupation, deaf to the overtures of the Vichy government, working by himself and apparently disconnected from what was happening. Only apparently; for although Braque, so little given to public declarations and manifestations, was not a committed artist, he was and would continue to be a *present* artist. Without losing sight of the painter's works and statements, this deserves some examination. From about 1938 or 1939 we may see in him, in certain still lifes and in the first works of the *Vanitas* series, the expression of a disquiet and a disenchanted metaphysical questioning that are characteristic of the period. At this time, too, in his replies to a survey conducted by Georges Duthuit on the influence of historical events on artistic creation, Braque agreed that the artist is "influenced, troubled and even more by history," but added that "ideas enter into his work only as driving forces. They have only a very indirect connection with the expression of quality and may well disappear when the painter looks at his canvas.... Whether we express serenity, therefore, or, on the contrary, disquiet, it happens without our knowledge" (*Cahiers d'Art*, Nos. 1-4, 1939). But it is not for purely aesthetic reasons that an artist in 1939 puts an unfurled French flag at the top of the mast of a beached boat (*The Boat with the Flag*). After the war Braque was to be more affirmative: "No artist, whoever he is and wherever he is, no representative artist escapes his time.... Even if he tries to escape from it, he is totally in it" (Recorded by André Verdet in *Georges Braque*, 1956). Even if, of course, his art prevailed, we shall see how the tragedy of the war years is often readable in Braque's work.

The *Vanitas* series was to continue throughout the war. Taken as it is, *Still Life with Skull*, which he began in 1941, is a gripping work: against a background of purple tones the skull stands out very clearly in front of some vaguer but identifiable objects that, despite the scant enthusiasm hitherto shown by Braque for symbolism, can nonetheless be perceived more or less as symbols: the imposing presence of death against the less assured, hazier presence of the spiritual world (the cross, a religious sign) and the material world (a vase of flowers, an object decorated with a bird). The message of prudence of a man who, unlike such other painters as Picasso, Léger, Chagall, or Rouault, kept political, religious, or other ideas at a distance. He had, moreover, announced his credo in plain language: "Never swear allegiance." But the war was a particular, and very hard, circumstance. Should we consider only in its formal aspects a picture like *The Two Mullets*, painted in 1940-41, undoubtedly a very sad period in Braque's life, a picture to which he remained sufficiently attached to keep it in his personal collection? How can we help thinking that the two little fish side by side on a plate, which somebody is about to eat with a dash of lemon, are two threatened beings, and that the large M on the pitcher may not be without its significance (it might possibly mean *aime*, or again it might be M for Marcelle, the painter's wife)? Braque had already painted fish once or twice during the Cubist period; their glistening scales presented an interesting problem for the young painter. But the fish that Braque was now painting—two together more often than not—were generally black (*Carafe and Fish*, 1941; *The Black Fish; Black Pitcher with Fish*, 1942), and this peculiarity has attracted a lot of attention. Each viewer must decide for himself whether to agree with Reverdy in seeing in this a personal image: "For me these black fish are a strong, moving image which I could not have invented myself or brought to life" (*Une aventure méthodique*, 1950); or whether to see in it, as Aragon did during the Resistance, a circumstanced symbol, that of imprisoned beings still aspiring to freedom: "Little streaks of gold, little streaks of grey; / In the deep blue water where the day is caught / The heavy black fish dream of the open sea" (*Le nouveau crève-cœur*, 1943-48). That the painter may not have thought of this interpretation does not exclude the possibility of others doing so. Neither of these explanations contradicts the beautiful canvas with its deep blacks, in which the only real clearness is that of the water in the carafe. When Braque reappeared before the general public at the 1943 Salon d'automne, showing *Still Life with Loaf, The Coffeepot,* and *The Blue Basin* (1941-42), the visitors may perhaps have seen in those works a celebration of the most everyday objects (which in fact they sometimes had to do without in those days); but in the large picture entitled *Patience*, depicting a woman with an anguished face brooding over a card game, how could they fail to see a message of hope and at the same time both the card game of the title (a game of solitaire) and the virtue they needed in those difficult times (patience). It is most improbable that a man so careful with words as Braque should not have intended this.

However that may have been, Braque decidedly did not want to be a man of ideas. His essential concern remained painting: the *Man with Easel* is looking at his picture, not at the public. He never ceased to work out his effects. Both in *The Blue Basin* (1942) and in *The Green Cloth* (1943), the white of the canvas appears at the joins of the planes of color, or else it is the black of the charcoal, since the paint has been very quickly brushed on, while at a little distance what might have been light—the window panes behind the earthenware service, the stained glass behind the green tablecloth—are on the contrary rendered in a very thick, uneven impasto, which considerably increases their luminosity. "In painting," Braque said, "the contrast of materials plays as important a role as the contrast of colors. I take advantage of all the differences and then the color takes on a much deeper meaning" (Interview with Dora Vallier). This was an old quest of his, one that he had been engaged on since his first use of sand and papiers collés.

At this moment when his painting seemed to be becoming more figurative again, Braque found himself diversifying his themes, which was something that he did not habitually worry about. The rural world makes an appearance: the 1943 *Still Life with Ladder* represents a corner of a barn or a cowshed; curiously perched on a ladder are a pitcher that seems to have strayed out of another picture and a fowl of some sort with its head downwards, pecking at something; in the shade behind some indefinite objects we see the head of a calf and that of a cow, whose large eyes glow comically in the darkness. Along with some little sculptures of animals that Braque did at about the same time, this is his first manifestation of affection for animals. Likewise rural is *My Bike* (begun in 1941, taken up again later, and finally completed in 1960!), which shows a bicycle emerging from a bush, a vision in which the only thing that looks real is the key in the door. The painter has added to the humor of the picture by surrounding it with a painted frame on which a roughly drawn cartouche proudly announces, in a single word, *Monvélo* (Mybike).

With the liberation of Normandy and Paris in 1944, Braque turned his attention to more playful themes, like flowers and billiard tables. He was to paint bouquets and billiards until 1952; one cannot imagine two lines more opposed and yet, without any doubt, complementary. However varied they may be, the bouquets are always very brightly colored and elegant, so much so that at times they seem conventional; they partake of the world of light. The *Billiard Tables*, on the contrary, are objects in a closed world of unemphasized colors under artificial lighting and are creations for calculation and play: rectangular for anybody looking at them, but full of angles and rebounds for the person playing. And with what a nerve the sixty-year-old painter played! The 1944 *Billiard Table* in the Musée National d'Art Moderne in Paris, which rears up and breaks in two, stupefied me when I was an adolescent, and thirty years later my stupefaction is still the same. Just after the war, halfway between the sensible arrangements of flowers and the boldness of the billiard tables, Braque was to embark on a series of *Garden Chairs* and *Terraces* that continued until well into the fifties. One of the most accomplished of the *Terraces*, though begun in 1948, was not considered by the painter to be really finished until 1961; but then Georges Limbour has warned us: "He is a man who has that serene force, a man *who has* time" (*Le Point*, October 1953). He also had behind him the time of all his accumulated experience, which, even if each new picture was a new experiment, gave weight to his *presence*. In *The Terrace*, against a background of panels in painted imitation wood that are worthy of the years 1912-14, we find capricious interlacings, trelliswork, and hatching borrowed from more recent research, all forming garden chairs and tables. The ballet of lines, forms, and colors, which in turn follow each other, are juxtaposed or wander off on their own account, already announces the *Studio* series, which was perhaps the greatest work of the painter's later years.

The great exhibition devoted to his work by the Galerie Maeght in 1947 was only a provisional assessment, for Braque now redoubled his activity. In 1948 he decided to publish his *Cahiers 1917-1947*, the notes and impressions that he had recorded over the years, the definitive edition of which was to come out in 1952 under the title *Le jour et la nuit*. These notes are rather laconic, the longest no more than a few lines, and reading them we understand Braque's fondness for the aphorisms of Heraclitus. These notes, from which I have frequently quoted in my text and which are indispensable for any intimate approach to the painter's work, are neither personal confidences nor commentaries on art and painting. Braque assures us that "the paint knows the picture better than the painter;" and so he lets the paint speak for him, being just as averse to theorizing as his friend Picasso. It was also around this time that Braque returned to engraving, which he had rather neglected after the *Theogony*, and did etchings or lithographs to illustrate books by his friends: Jean Paulhan, Pierre Reverdy, René Char, Francis Ponge....

STUDIOS, BIRDS, PLOWS

In 1949 Braque began the series of the *Studios*. He worked on it for nearly eight years, developing almost simultaneously a theme that was to come from it, that of the *Birds*. The *Studio* series consists of eight large canvases. The first six were painted between 1949 and 1952, and the last two between 1952 and 1956, the theme of the birds having become independent between the two parts of the series. By their very theme, the *Studios* take us into the painter's most intimate world, the place where he works

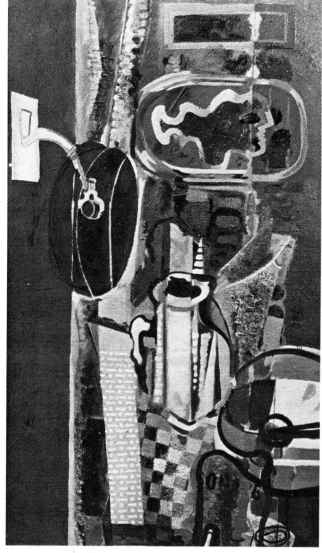

Studio V. 1949-50. Oil on canvas, 130×74 cm.
Private collection, New York.

and reflects, and in some ways the interior of his art. And thus we gain some idea of the importance they possessed in his eyes and their essential place in his *œuvre*. Since there is no simple way of summing up half a century of life and art ("With increasing age, art and life become one," Braque noted), these pictures are of a real complexity, not to say esotericism, that the painter has not sought to avoid. This also means that in their conception and form there is no place for logic and its conventions, and that any "explanations" could only be reductive. Here I shall not attempt to give any more than a skimming, superficial account of the series, without any pretensions to a deeper study.

The general shape of the studio makes it a closed world, in which the absence of a horizon probably suits Braque very well. At the same time it has much of the landscape about it, since it occupies a fairly large space, and also something of the still life on account of the objects accumulated in it. This latest intention, therefore, was not an entirely new idea for Braque, if we remember the sections of studios that appeared in the Cubist canvases, the *Mantelpiece* series during the twenties and, closer still owing to the opening of their angle, certain paintings done at the end of the thirties, such as *Studio with Black Vase* or *The Painter and His Model*. Thus the space has gradually grown larger around the still lifes and has been recentered around the painter, or more exactly around his work. At the beginning, moreover, in *Studio I* (1949), it

is only this work that appears, for the objects consist of hardly more than a few pictures and frames, and a painting or lithograph on the wall. For this reason the structure of the picture is simply based on rectangular planes: a wall painted with the "comb" technique, moldings and skirting boards, work on paper stuck on the wall, and in front of all of this, not even interrupted by the shape of a piece of a palette or a table, the pictures, one of them perfectly centered and visible, like a picture within the picture. Perhaps by coincidence, the light-colored shape between the pitcher and the plate of fruit resembles a bird with outspread wings. The work, however, gives us no inkling of what is to follow.

Studio II, also painted in 1949, differs from its predecessor in being extremely cluttered and based on a certain confusion of forms increased even more by a rain of verticals through the whole picture. Three types of object are juxtaposed: the painter's tools (easel, palette), the familiar objects, whether painted or not (fruit dish, lamp, jar), and representations, whether from a picture or not (a head independently sculpted or taken from an incised plaque). But there is also, traversing the clutter of lines and forms like a ghost, a great, serene bird. It is no longer visible in *Studio III* (1949-50), but this work in a high, narrow format is a return to the more realistic world of *Studio I*, keeping the general shape of the room and an appreciable depth thanks to the effect of rounded objects in a setting of pronounced angles. *Studio IV* (1949) takes us back to the structure of the second picture, but with less clutter: the tools, the familiar objects, and the objects of art are less numerous and more visible; the background, too, is simplified into a window (closed, of course). Despite the presence of a large easel, it is a huge bird that attracts our whole attention; it is no longer caught in the vertical lines, but visibly breaks them. This bird, neither painted nor sculpted, must nonetheless have a direct relationship with painting, for it has taken on the form of the palette. The presence of the bird becomes even more noticeable in *Studio V* (1949-51), inasmuch as the clutter of the space increases to a point at which the objects in it are not always discernible and the background in turn becomes decidedly turbulent with its overlapping surfaces. Alone, calm and unambiguous, the bird passes through this suffocation of signs and objects, which it bumps into without taking the slightest heed. A sixth picture, *Studio VI*, will bring back some apparent order, but only the better to disconcert us with a sort of confrontation between the bird and the easel, which has assumed for the occasion the form of an octopus—and strutting across the picture, quite clear and wholly realistic, there is a little white chicken whose presence is absolutely disconcerting.

What was the painter getting at in this fascinating story of the appearance of a bird? But if the pictures are fascinating, surely that is all that matters? We should recall with Braque that "art is made to disquiet," and that "there is only one thing valid in art: the one that cannot be explained." For the rest we need only remember to what an extent space was a constant preoccupation of Braque's as a painter. Is there a body freer in space than that of a bird? Is a bird not the most complete antithesis possible of the static, closed, well-considered world of the painter's studio? And if one says that a bird is a form, a movement in space, is one speaking of a bird or of painting?

Braque had not yet finished with the question, for in 1953 he signed and exhibited a seventh picture in which, as in *Studio VIII*, the bird has been extricated from the entanglement of the external forms in which it was hitherto imprisoned and is more or less contained, held, in the frame of a picture behind it. We know nothing of *Studio VII* except from photographs or what can be guessed from the following works, for Braque was dissatisfied with this picture and revised it entirely for what was to be the last in the series, *Studio IX* (1952-56). Unlike its predecessors, *Studio IX* is square; the tools and objects to which the other pictures have accustomed us are certainly still there, but their form or their position is disconcerting; in what is perhaps the rectangle of a fireplace there is a large steaming cauldron on which (or in which) we see the form of a fruit dish. Let us be careful not to speak of magic or alchemy, for Braque has put us on our guard (''Magic is the ensemble of means created by credulity''). And yet the great bird of the other *Studios* is no longer the imposing form on a single support that it was: it has been shattered into several bodies and fragments, as though by the brush of a Cubist or a Futurist. It has become pure dynamics, effects of colors in the sunlight (or the moonlight?). Wholly bathed in a penumbra of browns and blues, pierced with yellow and pink, the work is at once marvellously enigmatic and significant of ''the immensity of his inner world,'' as was so pleasantly said by Jean Louis Ferrier (*La petite forme*, 1985) in speaking of these works.

When Braque finished his last *Studio*, he was already in the middle of a period of birds that was not to end until his death. He himself examined the history of his relations with the theme: ''It was in 1929 that this motif appeared to me for an illustration of Hesiod. In 1910 I had painted birds, but they were incorporated in still lifes, whereas in my latest things I have been haunted by space and movement'' (interview with Jean Leymarie, *Quadrum*, 5, 1958). We must indeed distinguish between Braque's new interest in birds and whatever interest he may have had in them before: those he engraved or fashioned in relief on plaques in 1939 were posed, as was the bird perched on a rung in the 1943 *Still Life with Ladder*. But what caught his interest in the early fifties was the winged being, master of space. He was not to attempt to copy the bird's flight, nor yet to render that flight by kinetic procedures like the chronophotography of the engineer Marey or the Futurist Balla's linked series. Closer to Brancusi in his method, he sought to render movement in space without any concern for realism, *through form*. It was birds he chose to figure on the ceiling of the Salle Henri II in the Louvre when he was given the chance to decorate it in 1952: a small number of birds surrounded by simple forms, a principle from which he was not to depart. The large 1960 canvas entitled *The Birds* is close to the composition on the Louvre ceiling in its sobriety: two silhouettes, one black and one white, circling over a tripartite background in clear and yet discreet colours. At the thought that such birds fly over the Etruscan potteries in the Louvre without disturbing them, Georges Limbour very rightly said that what was required was ''a great deal of tact, humility and imagination'' (*Le Point*, October 1953).

In simplifying the form of the bird, Braque does not make it an ideal being. Though rarely differentiated according to species, the bird remains a body with weight—but a dynamic one, as we may see from the couples in *Birds in Flight* (1959), streamlined by their sharp, tapering forms, but terrestrial in their color and their granular texture against the sky, although the sky is painted thickly and heavier than they. As it approaches the earth, the bird remains a simple and simply colored form, but in flight—the very beautiful 1955 picture *The Bird and Its Nest* shows an animal with wings outspread, the thin line of whose eye accentuates its dynamism; its form is echoed in its nest, which, with its oblong eggs, is like a sun with closed eyes. If by space Braque's birds are linked to light, to the sun, to fire, that does not mean that they are phoenixes. They live and die, and in Braque's

The Bird and Its Nest. 1955. Oil on canvas, 130.5 × 173.5 cm. Musée National d'Art Moderne, Paris.

works, when they do not fly it means that they are dead: *The Dead Bird* (1957) becomes realistic, we can see its round eye, its hanging head, its feet, its motionless wings, and even the detail of its tail feathers, but it is only the black form of a dead animal. Birds have been painted or sculpted often enough, and yet those of Braque, in their freshness and freedom, give the impression of a new theme. As Saint-John Perse has said, ''Not being sign or symbol, but the thing itself in its fact and its fatality... they have not frequented the world of myth or legend'' (*Oiseaux*, 1963). They are not born from the fire, they do not bear olive branches, which justifies Rebecca West's rather cruel remark: ''Picasso's dove of peace is an eminently political bird; in the sky that it traverses, its wings inscribe slogans intended for mankind's attention. But Braque's birds are simply birds that fly for the pleasure of flying'' (*Verve*, 31-32, 1955).

Among the many birds painted by Braque the most singular is certainly the large one in *In Full Flight*. First exhibited in 1956, this canvas showed, in a very blue grainy sky, a powerful, slender bird flying into a great mass thatc, although heavy, was as black and gleaming as the bird itself, and which must have been a cloud. Dissatisfied with his work as he often was, Braque took back his picture and painted in the corner a surprising enclave repeating the outline of a duck in full flight, which he had already used before. The little picture thus included inverts the values of the large one; the bird in it is white and is leaving the black to enter the blue. In 1961 Braque exhibited a corrected version. But let the painter himself explain the reasons for this change: ''After four months, observing it every day, living it, I realized that it had become too habitual for me, too great a comfort for my eye. And so I decided to create a break by painting in the lower left-hand corner of the picture another bird delimited by a sort of rectangular white frame, the whole placed there like a marginal note, or even a stamp. By creating the contradiction, and not the discord, the whole picture lives in a more unusual way. One sometimes needs surprise. It prevents one from settling into a routine'' (Recorded by André Verdet, 1978). The whole of Braque is in this last reflection, astonishing only for those who see him as a stay-at-home painter, always ready to trot out the same themes.

The fact that I have lingered over these major series should not lead anyone to think that at that time Braque was painting nothing but studios or birds. No more than at any other period did the fact that these were essential preoccupations for him prevent him from continuing to deal with other themes and to use other techniques (litho-

Plow in the Sun. 1958. Oil on canvas, 37 × 57 cm.
Private collection.

graphy, sculpture, ceramics...). Nor does the fact that they were different mean that the work he did at the same time was necessarily secondary. As proof of this I need only mention some large canvases painted at the time of the *Studio* series, such as *Night* (1951) or *Ajax* (1954), which were a return to the inspiration of mythology in Braque's work. The first shows a horned woman emerging from the bushy chaos of darkness, tall and proud as Artemis; the second is a fine warrior worked in tortuous lines and Greek frets to mark infinity. Or else some subject very obviously of our own century, such as the *Bicycle* (1961-62), which he succeeds in making as timeless and beautiful as a fossil imprint on stone. In a minor register, there is a still life—flowers or an aquarium in which he was interested in the way the diffraction of the glass split or distorted the images of fish...

Seascapes and shore scenes also continued to attract him, with their boats, rocks, and pebbles. His seascapes are perhaps more somber than earlier works and display a thicker, more tortured impasto. But one would be wrong to infer from that any sort of pessimism in the aging painter. Around this time, perhaps to escape occasionally from the introverted world of the *Studios*, he also returned, beyond the cliffs along the coast, to the Norman countryside, which is like a prolongation of the sea, with its vast fields stretching away out of sight. He had not painted it for nearly half a century. Georges Limbour gives us a judicious explanation of this: "The wind, the clouds, the sudden lights, ebb and flow, everything changes in a moment: it is the country of mobility. It was this that Braque had chosen; it was for this that he had long before given up Provence and its unmoving light" (*Le Point*, October 1953). If the younger Braque had indeed been fascinated by the static quality of things in space, it was changing space that attracted him now. It was this quality of movement that appealed to him in those broad canvases like the *Landscape with Somber Sky* (1955) or *The Rape Field* (1956-57): the swirlings of a clear or stormy sky, the

waving of plants in the wind. It was not the nuances of the atmosphere, however, that held his attention; he was not an Impressionist. As in his Cubist days, he remained a realist. And his painting evidences his deep-rooted materialism: the fat land and the warmth of the colors of the fields brought out by a thick, mobile, sensuous touch, painting as "with a full hand." His words come back to us now: "Impelled by the desire to go further in the manifestation of space.... I wanted to make the touch a form of matter" (Interview with Dora Vallier). The canvas is skimmed over, brushed, patted; it is left bare, or the paint forms little heaps on it....

In a canvas like *Landscape with Somber Sky*, we see in the foreground the wheel and handles of a plow, the low shadow of which stretches in the light of the evening with a storm rising. For some time, in fact, plows had been present in Braque's work; in the evening of his life they were to be ubiquitous. Of some of his still lifes Francis Ponge could say: "Nothing anecdotal, but always, more or less, an example, a law, a device, an emblem" (*Nouveau recueil*, 1967). That was exactly what it was: treated with sweeping strokes of color applied with a knife in a large-scale painting such as the 1960 *Large Plow*, or with diffused stippling in a small format like that of *The Plow* (1961), it was an emblem that came from matter and time. They are in the stones, in the flowers, in the snow or in a corner of a field, but they are only waiting for their moment to serve. They are impressive, whatever their form or their color: the red turnwrest with its double share is as fragile as a skiff and the blue-black fixed-furrow is as stubby as a mole, but they all have the function of advancing in the soil, scouring down into it and leaving a trace. The earth is their abode. It was not about them that the painter said in 1961: "I have plowed my furrow and advanced, slowly, in the same research.... A line of continuity" (Interview with André Verdet). And yet....

It has been said that the last canvas signed by Braque showed a plow; and when he died, in the middle of the summer of 1963, his last work was a little canvas: a simple corner of a pedestal table with a vase, some fruit and flowers, which he left unfinished. The land, fruits and industry of man that Braque celebrated in his painting, present in the things of the earth to the last.

Braque's world is large, open and yet modest, unemphatic, sometimes secret. One does not enter it as though it were a mill, and certainly not as though it were a conquered country: the evidence is not essential, the friendship of a work is only won by those who deserve it. Braque's lesson is that of a great and humble artist. Let us remember that a sympathetic eye sees better than a critical eye and that neither the intuitive nor the rational approaches exhaust the possibilities of a work: "A good picture never ceases to give of itself." Since he has also told us that "art is made to disquiet," let us not complain that we are sometimes disconcerted: it is much better so. Let us take our time. ...

The lesson of the great works of art is always the same.

BIOGRAPHY

1882. Birth of Georges Braque, in Argenteuil-sur-Seine, on 13 May. He is the son of Charles Braque, a house painter and builder, and his wife, Augustine Johannet.

1890. Charles Braque moves to Le Havre with all his family. There Georges Braque spends his childhood and adolescence without any remarkable incidents.

1893. Begins his secondary schooling at the Lycée in Le Havre.

1897. Attends the evening courses at the School of Fine Arts and is given flute lessons by one of Dufy's brothers, his family not opposing his penchant for art. Meets two other young painters, Raoul Dufy and Othon Friesz. "I have always had a sensibility to painting. My father, who was a building contractor, loved to paint in his spare time. My grandfather, too, had been a keen amateur painter. I myself was born in Argenteuil, just at the time when the Impressionists were working there. And it was in Le Havre, again in a totally Impressionist atmosphere, that I spent my childhood" (G. Braque).

1899. Gives up his secondary studies, goes into his father's business and is later apprenticed to Roney, a painter and decorator.

1900. Goes to Paris to continue his apprenticeship with another painter and decorator, Laberthe. Lodges in the rue des Trois Frères in Montmartre. Enrolls in the municipal art courses of Les Batignolles. His friends Friesz and Dufy are also in Paris, but they are enrolled in Léon Bonnat's courses at the School of Fine Arts.

1901-02. Does his military service in the infantry, at Le Havre, but never neglects an opportunity to paint when he can (portraits of relatives, landscapes).

1903. Attends Bonnat's courses at the School of Fine Arts for two months, then returns to the Académie Humbert.

1904. Spends the summer in Normandy and Brittany. On his return to Paris, rents a studio in the rue d'Orsel. Few canvases from this period have survived.

1905. Spends the summer working in Honfleur and Le Havre, in the company of the sculptor Manolo and the critic Maurice Raynal. At the Salon d'automne, where his friends Dufy and Friesz are exhibiting, he is impressed by the painting of Matisse and Derain.

1906. In March, exhibits for the first time (seven pictures) at the Salon des Indépendants. Spends a month in Antwerp with Friesz, returns to Paris (where he spends September and October), then stays at L'Estaque from November 1906 to January 1907; all these months are decisive, for it is during them that his first Fauvist pictures are painted.

1907. Returning to Paris in February, exhibits six paintings at the Salon des Indépendants. Meets Matisse, Derain, and Vlaminck. During the summer, returns to the Midi, staying first at La Ciotat and then at L'Estaque. The young art dealer Daniel-Henry Kahnweiler and Guillaume Apollinaire show interest in his work. It is the latter who takes him to the studio in the Bateau-Lavoir occupied by Picasso, whose paintings surprise him. The exhibitions devoted to Cézanne at the Salon d'automne and at the Galerie Bernheim-Jeune prove equally impressive. In December, begins to work on his *Large Nude*.

1908. A banquet is held at Picasso's studio in honor of the Douanier Rousseau, the food and entertainment being entrusted to Fernande Olivier; among the more notable guests are Braque, Apollinaire, Max Jacob, André Salmon, Maurice Raynal, Marie Laurencin, and Leo and Gertrude Stein. Spends the spring and summer at L'Estaque. Despite Marquet's support, the jury of the Salon d'automne refuses his paintings. D. H. Kahnweiler offers him his gallery, and there, in November, Braque's first one-man show is held, with a presentation by Apollinaire: "Georges Braque does not know what repose is, and each of his pictures is a monument to an endeavor which nobody before him had ever attempted." It is in front of these canvases that people in Paris first begin to talk of *Cubism*.

1909. Spends the summer working at La Roche-Guyon and Carrières-Saint-Denis. Becomes more closely connected with Picasso (André Salmon).

1910. Rents a new studio in the rue Caulaincourt. Spends the summer at L'Estaque. At this period, when the "Picasso gang" used to go down from Montmartre to visit people like the Steins, for instance, Braque was always on the bus, "playing the accordion to enliven the journey" (André Salmon).

1911. Spends the summer at Céret with Picasso. In the picture entitled *The Portuguese*, introduces stenciled letters and digits. Becomes friendly with the scuptor Henri Laurens and the poet Pierre Reverdy. "I am sorry for those who have lived through this marvelous period but have made no effort to communicate either the frequently discouraging trials of their lives at that time or the incomparable surge of emotion and spiritual happiness. I doubt whether there has ever been so much blue sky and sun in the history of art, so much responsibility heroically shouldered, so great a distance between hope and disaster, so much courage and so many sudden frights between success and failure" (Pierre Reverdy).

1912. Exhibits in Cologne (*Sonderbund*), Munich (*Blaue Reiter*) and Prague, and meets the Italian Futurists who have arrived in Paris. Marries Marcelle Lapré. Spends the summer in Sorgues with Picasso and Reverdy. Does some sculptures in paper. First papiers collés and inclusions of sand, sawdust, etc., in his painting. When Picasso returns to Paris, he writes to Braque: "I am using your latest paper and dust processes."

1913. Participates in the celebrated Armory Show in New York. In June, visits Picasso, Juan Gris, and Max Jacob at Céret, then goes on to Sorgues and works there until November. Apollinaire publishes *Les peintres cubistes*: "And now we come to Georges Braque. His role has been a heroic one. His serene art is admirable. His endeavors are always serious."

1914. Is called up while at Sorgues and sent to join the 224th infantry regiment.

1915. Is wounded near Carency on 11 May. "Second Lieutenant Braque, with a wound in the head, was left for dead on the battlefield of Neuville-Saint-Vaast. The next day he was picked up by the stretcher-bearers. After trepanation, Braque spent two days in a coma, recovering consciousness on his birthday, 13 May 1915" (Jean Paulhan). His friends are greatly shocked to hear that he has been so seriously wounded. "Oh, our Braque! That robust man, painter and soldier, with bleeding brow! (André Salmon). Spends his convalescence at Sorgues. Posted for a time to the Bernay depot in the Eure, is finally invalided out.

1916. After demobilization, spends his time between Paris and Sorgues, but is as yet unable to paint.

1917. On 15 January his friends hold a banquet to celebrate his cure; does not begin to paint again, however, until the summer. Is then very close to Laurens, Juan Gris, and Reverdy. In his review *Nord-Sud*, Reverdy publishes Braque's *Pensées et réflexions sur la peinture*.

1918. Does the first still lifes with pedestal tables and clarinets. Two drawings for Pierre Reverdy's *Les ardoises du toit*.

1919. In March, exhibits at the Galerie de l'Effort Moderne, run by his new dealer, Léonce Rosenberg. "Georges Braque is a pure spirit. He has only one thing in his head: quality" (Blaise Cendrars).

1920. Does three woodcuts for Erik Satie's *Le piège de Méduse*. This book is published by Kahnweiler (Galerie Simon), now back in Paris after having had to leave it on account of being a German citizen. Braque does his first sculpture since the pre-war structures in paper: *Femme debout*. Roger Bissière publishes the first little monograph on his work.

1921. During the three years when the property of D. H. Kahnweiler impounded during the war is publicly sold, many works by Braque are dispersed. Braque is very dissatisfied with Léonce Rosenberg, who has been appointed as the expert for these sales, and terminates his contract with him. "Braque's admirable papiers collés and canvases stimulated the buyers. They were the works of his great period, the most moving and tender that I know by this grave painter who respects the mysteries" (Robert Desnos). Braque takes an interest in the latest avant-garde movements but, finding them excessive, remains somewhat aloof; the newcomers do not hold it against him. "Braque used to look at one fixedly. His great height was impressive, and even more so his hands, which were very large, the hands of a craftsman. He spoke very little, hardly at all" (Philippe Soupault). "I only met Braque once, for a couple of minutes, but I found him rather likable" (Ezra Pound). It is Louis Aragon who is to buy the 1907-08 *Large Nude*.

1922. Exhibits eighteen works, among them *The Canephorae*, in the room of honor at the Salon d'automne. Leaves Montmartre to settle in Montparnasse.

1924. In Monte Carlo, on 19 January, premiere of the Diaghilev ballet company's production of *Les Fâcheux*, to music by Georges Auric and with décor and costumes by Braque. Exhibits at the gallery of Paul Rosenberg, his new dealer. In Paris, on 17 May, premiere of the Comte de Beaumont ballet company's production of *Salade*: music by Darius Milhaud, décor and costumes by Braque. Has a house built for him at No. 6 in the rue du Douanier (now the rue Georges-Braque) by the architect Auguste Perret: "A private road was opened on the avenue du Parc Montsouris. And private houses, built by happy painters, gave a proud air to this little street, called the rue du Douanier in posthumous homage to our dear old Rousseau. Next door to each other, or almost, André Derain and Georges Braque..." (André Salmon).

1925. Creates the décor for the Diaghilev ballet company's production of *Zéphyr et Flore*. Visits Rome. Period of the *Chimneys* and the *Green Marble Table*.

1926. One-man show at the Galerie Paul Rosenberg.

1929. Spends the summer in Dieppe; is very pleased with this return to Normandy.

1931. Has a house built at Varengeville, near Dieppe. From now on is to divide his time between Paris and Varengeville. Visits Florence and Venice. Does his first work in incised plaster.

1932. Does sixteen etchings as illustrations for Ambroise Vollard's publication of Hesiod's *Theogony*.

1933. Has his first retrospective exhibition, organized by the Basel Kunsthalle. Special number of *Cahiers d'art* devoted to Braque.

1936. One-man show at the Palais des Beaux-arts in Brussels. Travels in Germany. Exhibition at the Galerie Paul Rosenberg.

1937. Is awarded the First Prize of the Carnegie Foundation in Pittsburg for *The Yellow Tablecloth*. In April, exhibition at the Galerie Paul Rosenberg, one of the most notable works presented being *The Painter and His Model*.

1939. Starts sculpting again. Travelling exhibition of works by Braque in the United States, beginning in November and continuing until March 1940 (Chicago, Washington, San Francisco).

1940. Fleeing from the German occupation, Braque takes refuge in the Limousin and later in the Pyrenees. At the end of the year is back in Paris and remains there working alone until the end of the War, deaf to the advances of the Vichy government.

1943. A room is reserved for him at the Salon d'automne; some of the works shown, like *Patience*, are not without ulterior significance.

1944. Beginning of the *Billiard Table* series: "In the future it will be said of this canvas that it is a Cubist reverie from the century of the great terror" (André Lhote).

1945. Undergoes a serious operation during the summer and has to give up his work for several months. His friends are a great support: "Picasso is one of the most faithful. He comes to spend the afternoon with us every other day" (Marcelle Braque). One-man show at the Stedelijk Museum in Amsterdan, then at the Palais des Beaux-arts in Brussels. Publication of Jean Paulhan's *Braque le patron*.

1946. Publication of *Braque le réconciliateur*, by Francis Ponge. Exhibits with Rouault at the Tate Galley, London.

1947. Exhibition at the gallery of Aimé Maeght, his new dealer.

1948. Publication of his notes, *Cahiers 1917-1947*: "Nothing in these notebooks, however, sheds the slightest light on Braque's private life, his passions, his ideas, his fantasies" (Rebecca West). First prize at the Venice Biennale for the 1944 *Billiard Table*.

1944. First paintings in the *Studio* series. Does four etchings to illustrate René Char's *Le soleil des eaux*. Retrospective in New York that goes on to Cleveland. Louis Jouvet commissions him to do the décor for his production of *Tartuffe*.

1959. Publication of Pierre Reverdy's *Une aventure méthodique*, an essay on Braque illustrated with lithographs.

1952. Retrospective exhibition in Tokyo.

1953. Paints three coffers for the ceiling in the Salle Henri II in the Louvre. Exhibition in Bern, going on to Zürich.

1954. Stained-glass windows for the chapel at Varengeville and for the church of Saint-Paul-de-Vence. Decorations for the Mas Bernard at Saint-Paul-de-Vence. Braque grants Dora Vallier an important interview for the review *Cahiers d'art*.

1956. Exhibition in Edinburgh, later presented in London. Exhibition at the Galerie Maeght.

1958. Retrospective exhibition in Rome. Exhibits (two rooms) at the Venice Biennale.

1959. Is obliged by illness to paint less, but does much drawing and engraving. Exhibition at the Galerie Maeght.

1960. Retrospective exhibition at the Kunsthalle, Basel. Does twelve lithographs to illustrate Reverdy's *La liberté des mers*.

1961. The Louvre Museum presents the exhibition "Braque's studio."

1962. Publication of *Oiseaux*, etchings by Braque with a text by Saint-John Perse: "Braque's succinctly drawn bird is no mere motif... It lives, moves, is consumed; concentration on being and constancy in being. It takes to itself, like a plant, the energy of light."

1963. Retrospective exhibition in Munich. On 31 August, Braque dies in Paris. Is accorded national honors, with a funeral oration delivered by André Malraux in the Cour carrée of the Louvre: "He is as rightfully at home in the Louvre as is the angel of Rheims in his cathedral." The burial takes place in Varengeville: "This wisdom is purely human, profoundly human, resolutely human, because it never appeals to, bows before, resigns itself to, adores or addresses prayers to any sort of transcendency—because it aims at nothing but pleasure, the absence of pain, and in judging of this refuses to be guided by anything but pure sensation..." (Francis Ponge).

BRIEF BIBLIOGRAPHY

Writings of Georges Braque

Cahiers de Georges Braque: 1917-1949. Maeght, Paris, 1949; new edition completed in 1956.
Le jour et la nuit. Gallimard, Paris, 1952.

On the Work of Georges Braque

APOLLINAIRE, Guillaume: *Les peintres cubistes*. Figuière, Paris, 1913.

ARAGON, Louis: *La peinture au défi*. Galerie Goemans, Paris, 1930.

BARR, Alfred: *Cubism and Abstract Art*. Museum of Modern Art, New York, 1936.

BISSIÈRE, Roger: *Georges Braque*. L'Effort Moderne, Paris, 1920.

BRUNET, Christian: *Braque et l'espace*. Klincksieck, Paris, 1971.

Cahiers d'Art, No. 1-2, special number devoted to Braque. Paris, 1933.

CASSOU, Jean: *Braque*. Flammarion, Paris, 1956.

CENDRARS, Blaise: *Aujourd'hui*. Graset, Paris, 1931.

CHARBONNIER, Georges: *Le monologue du peintre*. Julliard, Paris, 1959.

COGNIAT, Raymond: *Braque*. Flammarion, Paris, 1970.

COOPER, Douglas: *The Cubist Epoch*. Phaidon Press, New York, 1971.

CRESPELLE, Jean-Paul: *Les Fauves*. Ides et Calendes, Neuchâtel, 1962.

Derrière le miroir, special number in homage to Braque. Paris, 1964.

DESCARGUES, Pierre & CARRÀ, Massimo: *Braque 1908-1929*. Flammarion, Paris, 1973.

EINSTEIN, Carl: *Georges Braque*. Les Chroniques du jour, Paris, 1934.

FAUCHEREAU, Serge: *La révolution cubiste*. Denoël, Paris, 1982.

FRY, Edward: *Le cubisme*. La Connaissance, Brussels, 1968.

FUMET, Stanislas: *Braque*. Braun, Paris, 1945.

GIEURE, Maurice: *Georges Braque*. Tisné, Paris, 1956.

GOLDING, John: *Cubism 1907-1914*. Wittenborn, New York, 1959.

GRENIER, Jean: *Braque: Peintures 1909-1947*. Le Chêne, Paris, 1948.

KAHNWEILER, D.-H.: *Les années héroïques du cubisme*. Braun, Paris, 1950.

LASSAIGNE, Jacques: "Entretien avec Braque," in the catalogue of the exhibition *Les Cubistes*, Bordeaux-Paris, 1973.

LAUDE, Jean & WORMS DE ROMILLY, Nicole: *Braque: le Cubisme*. Maeght, Paris, 1982.

Le Point, special number devoted to Braque. Souillac, 1953.

LEYMARIE, Jean: *Braque*. Skira, Geneva, 1961.

LHOTE, André: *Les invariants plastiques*. Hermann, Paris, 1967.

LIMBOUR, Georges: *Dans le secret des ateliers*. L'Elocoquent, Paris, 1986.

MOURLOT, Fernand & PONGE, Francis: *Braque lithographe*. Sauret, Monte Carlo, 1963.

PAULHAN, Jean: *Braque le patron*, definitive edition. Gallimard, Paris, 1952.

PAULHAN, Jean: *La peinture cubiste*. Denoël-Gonthier, Paris, 1970.

PERSE, Saint-John: *Oiseaux*. Gallimard, Paris, 1963.

PONGE, Francis: *Le peintre à l'étude*. Gallimard, Paris, 1948.

PONGE, Francis, DESCARGUES, Pierre & MALRAUX, André: *G. Braque*. Draeger, Paris, 1971.

RAYNAL, Maurice: *Georges Braque*. Valori Plastici, Rome, 1921.

REVERDY, Pierre: *Une aventure méthodique*. Mourlot, Paris, 1950.

RICHARDSON, John: *Georges Braque*. Penguin Books, Armondsworth, 1959.

RUSSELL, John: *Georges Braque*. Phaidon, London, 1959.

SALMON, André: *Souvenirs sans fin*. 3 Volumes. Gallimard, Paris, 1955, 1956, 1961.

SEUPHOR, Michel: *L'œuvre graphique de Braque*. Berggruen, Paris, 1953.

TONO, Yoshiaki: *Picasso - Braque*. Zauho Press, Tokyo, 1967.

VALLIER, Dora: *L'intérieur de l'art*. Le Seuil, Paris, 1982.

VERDET, André: *Georges Braque*. Kister, Geneva, 1956.

Verve, No. 31-32, special number devoted to Braque. Paris, 1955.

ZERVOS, Christian: *Georges Braque: nouvelles sculptures et plaques gravées*. Morancé, Paris, 1960.

Catalogue Raisonné of Braque's Work

The catalogue raisonné of the paintings drawn up by Nicole Worms de Romilly is in the course of publication by Éditions Maeght, Paris; seven volumes have been published since 1959. For the period from 1906 to 1929, a first provisional catalogue drawn up by Georges Isarlov was published by Éditions José Corti in Paris in 1932.

The catalogue raisonné of the engravings drawn up by Dora Vallier was published by Éditions Flammarion in Paris in 1982.

1. *Grandmother's Friend*. c. 1900.
   Oil on canvas, 61 × 50 cm.
   Private collection.

1

2

3

2. *The Port of Le Havre*. Summer 1903.
   Wash drawing on paper.
   Private collection.

3. *The Port of Antwerp*. 1906.
   Oil on canvas, 38 × 46 cm.
   Von der Heydt Museum, Wuppertal.

4. *The Port of L'Estaque*. 1906.
   Oil on canvas, 37 × 46 cm.
   Private collection.

5. *The Port of Antwerp: the Mast*. 1906.
   Oil on canvas, 46 × 38 cm.
   Galerie Beyeler, Basel.

4

5

6

7

6. *Landscape near L'Estaque.* 1906.
   Oil on canvas, 59 × 72 cm.
   Musée National d'Art Moderne, Paris.

7. *Landscape near L'Estaque.* 1906.
   Oil on canvas, 50 × 61 cm.
   Private collection.

8. *Landscape near L'Estaque.* 1906.
   Oil on canvas, 60 × 72.5 cm.
   Private collection.

9. *View of L'Estaque from the Hotel Mistral.*
   1907.
   Oil on canvas, 81.5 × 61 cm.
   Josten Collection, New York.

8

9

10

11

10. *The Viaduct at L'Estaque*. 1907.
    Oil on canvas, 65 × 81 cm.
    The Minneapolis Institute of Art.

11. *Seated Nude Seen from Behind*. c. 1907.
    Oil on canvas, 55 × 46 cm.
    Musée National d'Art Moderne, Paris.

12. *Study for Nude*. 1907-08.
    Etching, 27.5 × 19.7 cm.
    Galerie Maeght, Paris.

13. *Landscape near L'Estaque*. 1908.
    Oil on canvas, 81 × 65 cm.
    Kunstmuseum, Basel.

12

13

14. *Large Nude.* 1907-08.
    Oil on canvas, 142 × 102 cm.
    Alex Maguy Collection, Paris.

15. *The Viaduct at L'Estaque.* 1908.
    Oil on canvas, 72.5 × 59 cm.
    Musée National d'Art Moderne, Paris.

16

17

16. *The Musical Instruments*. 1908.
    Oil on canvas, 50 × 61 cm.
    Private collection.

17. *The Metronome*. 1908-09.
    Oil on canvas, 41 × 33 cm.
    Statens Museum for Kunst, Copenhagen.

18. *Port in Normandy*. 1909.
    Oil on canvas, 81 × 81 cm.
    The Art Institute, Chicago.

19. *The Castle of La Roche-Guyon*. 1909.
Oil on canvas, 80×59.5 cm.
Moderna Museet, Stockholm.

20. *Pitcher, Bottle, Lemon*. 1909.
Oil on canvas, 46×38 cm.
Stedelijk Museum, Amsterdam.

21. *The Sacré-Coeur*. 1910.
Oil on canvas, 55.5×41 cm.
Musée d'Art Moderne du Nord, Villeneuve d'Asq.

22. *Little Cubist Guitar*. 1909-10.
Etching, 13×19.4 cm.
Galerie Maeght, Paris.

20

21

22

23. *Piano and Mandola*. 1909-10.
Oil on canvas, 92 × 42.5 cm.
The Guggenheim Museum, New York.

24. *Violin and Palette*. 1909-10.
Oil on canvas, 92 × 42.5 cm.
The Guggenheim Museum, New York.

25. *Still Life with Metronome*. 1910.
Oil on canvas, 81.5 × 53.5 cm.
Private collection.

23

24

26

27

26. *Woman with Mandolin*. 1910.
Oil on canvas, 91.5×72.5 cm.
Bayerische Staatsgemaldesammlung, Munich.

27. *Basket of Fish*. 1910-11.
Oil on canvas, 50.2×61 cm.
Museum of Art, Philadelphia.

28. *Paris 1910*. 1910-11.
Etching, 19.6×27.7 cm.
Galèrie Maeght, Paris.

29. *The Violin*. 1911.
Oil on canvas, 130×89 cm.
Musée National d'Art Moderne, Paris.

30. *The Candlestick*. 1911.
Oil on canvas, 46×38 cm.
Scottish Museum of Modern Art, Edinburgh.

29

30

28

31

31. *The Portuguese*. 1911.
    Oil on canvas, 117×81.5 cm.
    Kunstmuseum, Basel.

32. *Soda*. 1911.
    Oil on canvas, diameter, 36.2 cm.
    Museum of Modern Art, New York.

33. *The Violin, Mozart, Kubelick*. 1912.
    Oil on canvas, 46×61 cm.
    Private collection, Basel.

34. *Still Life with Cluster of Grapes
    (Fruit Dish, Bottle and Glass, Sorgues)*. 1912.
    Oil and sand on canvas, 60×73 cm.
    Private collection.

32

33

34

35. *The Guitar*. 1912.
   Papier collé, 70.2 × 60.7 cm.
   Private collection.

36. *Still Life "Valse"*. 1912.
   Oil and sand on canvas, 91.4 × 64.5 cm.
   Guggenheim Museum, Venice.

37. *The Violin*. 1912-1913.
   Oil on canvas, 81 × 65 cm.
   Württembergische Staatsgalerie, Stuttgart.

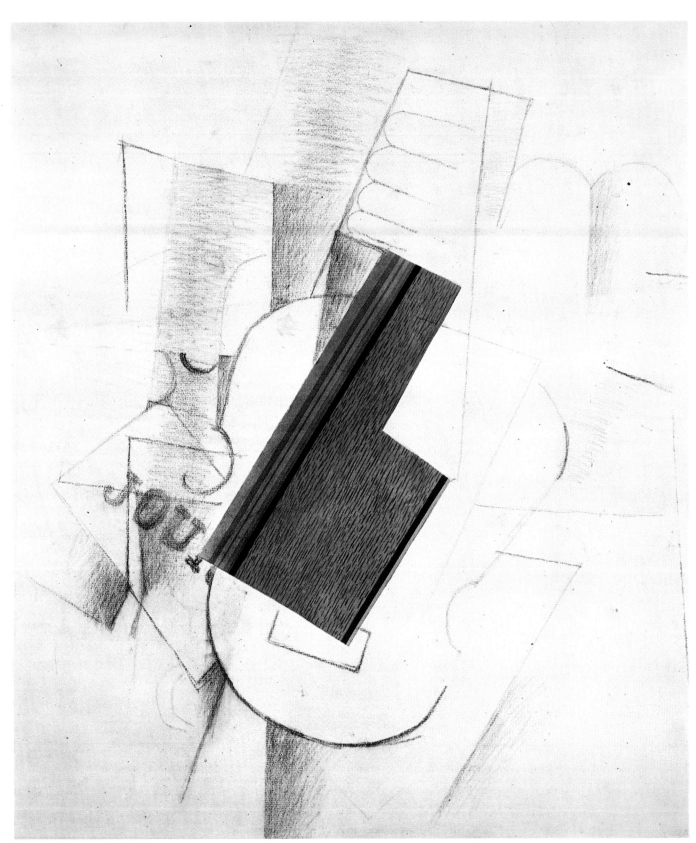

36

37

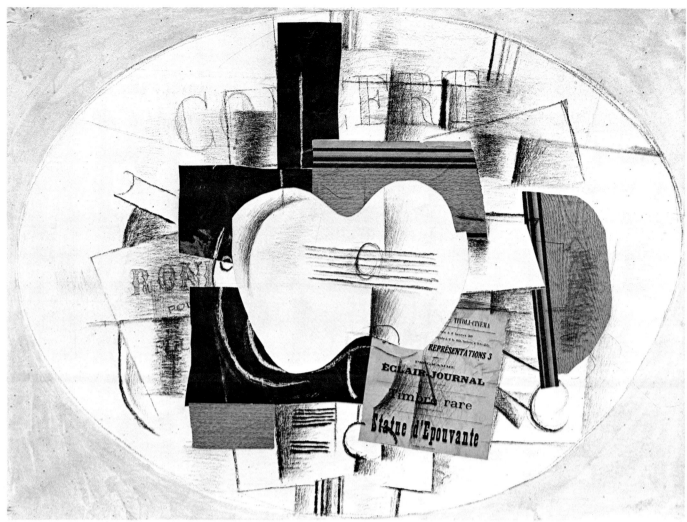

38

39

41

42

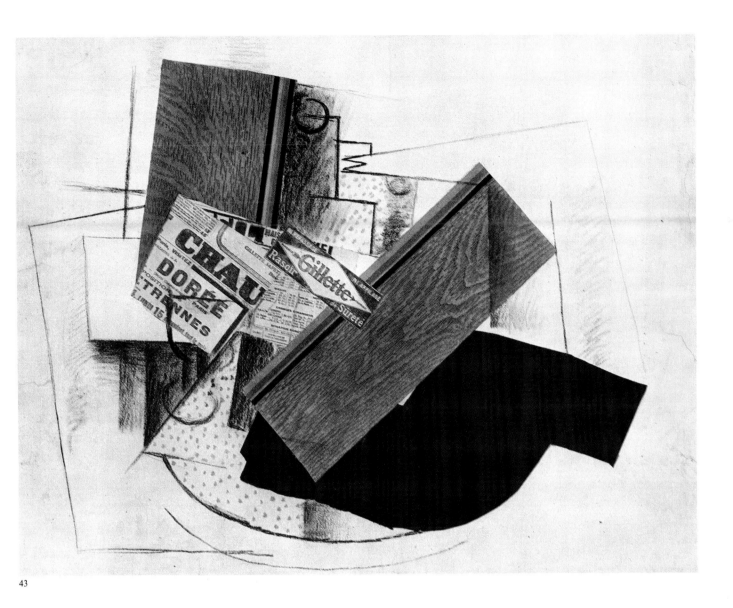

43

44

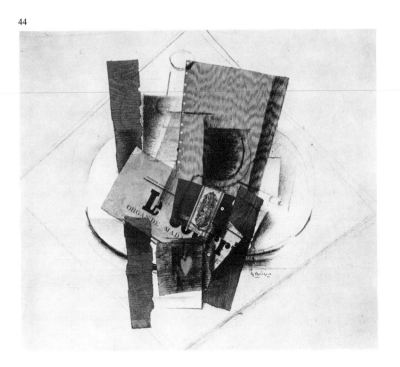

41. *Still Life with Glass and Newspaper*. 1913.
Oil on canvas, 91×71 cm.
Private collection.

42. *The Daily Paper (Violin and Pipe)*. 1913.
Papier collé, 74×106 cm.
Musée National d'Art Moderne, Paris.

43. *Still Life on the Table*. 1914.
Papier collé, 48×62 cm.
Musée National d'Art Moderne, Paris.

44. *The Post*. 1913.
Papier collé, 52×67 cm.
Museum of Art, Philadelphia. A. E. Gallatin collection.

45

45. *Glass, Violin and Music Paper
(The Violin, Valse)*. 1913.
Oil on canvas, 64.5 × 91.5 cm.
Walraf-Richartz Museum, Cologne.

46. *The Musician's Table*. 1913.
Oil on canvas, 65 × 92 cm.
Kunstmuseum, Basel.

47. *The Man with the Guitar*. 1914.
Oil on canvas, 130 × 73 cm.
Musée National d'Art Moderne, Paris.

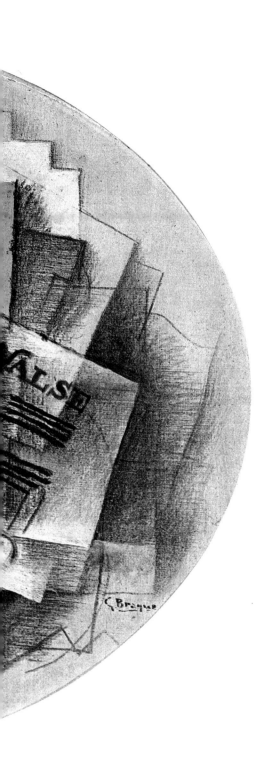

46

47

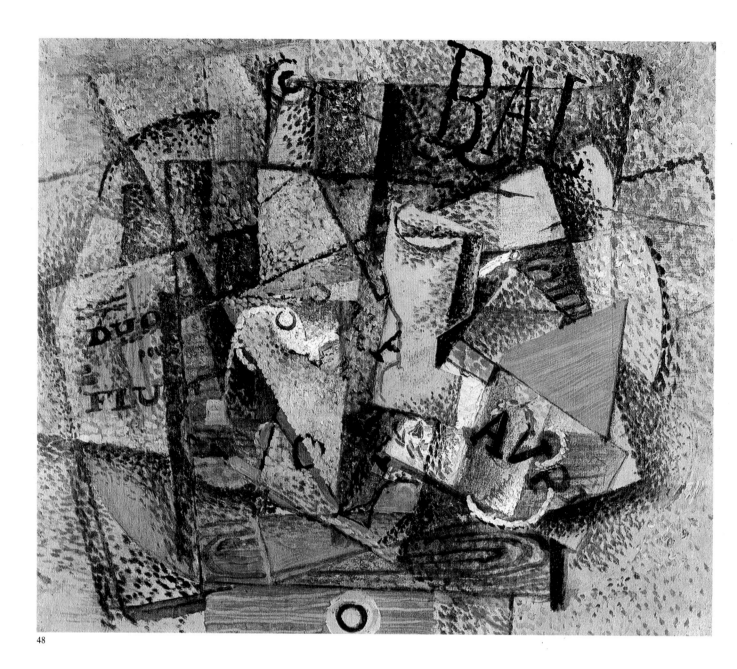

48

48. *Glass, Bottle and Pipe on a Table*. 1914.
Oil on canvas, 46×55 cm.
Mattioli Collection, Milan.

49. *The Ace of Hearts*. 1914.
Papier collé, 30×41 cm.
Private collection, Basel.

50. *The Mandolin*. 1914.
Gouache with paper and corrugated cardboard glued on,
50×32 cm.
Kunstmuseum, Ulm.

51. *Musical Instruments and Newspaper*. 1917-18.
Indian ink on paper, 35×19.5 cm.
Musée National d'Art Moderne, Paris.

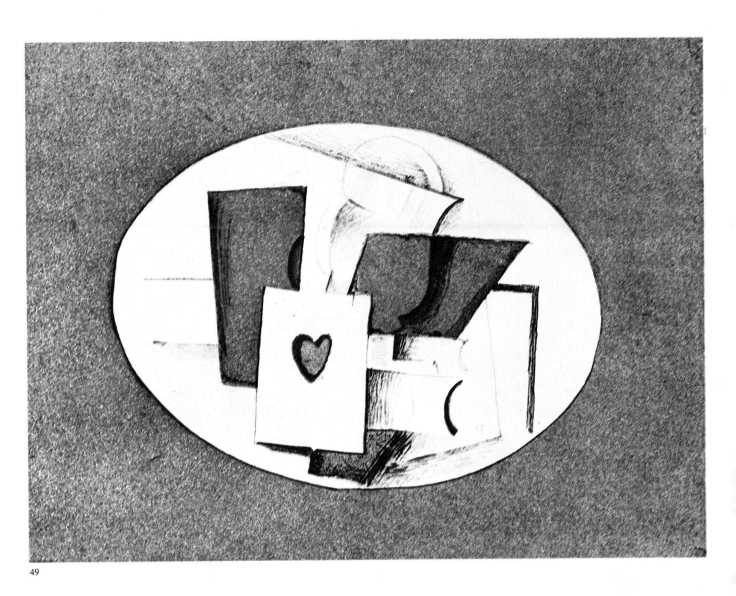

49

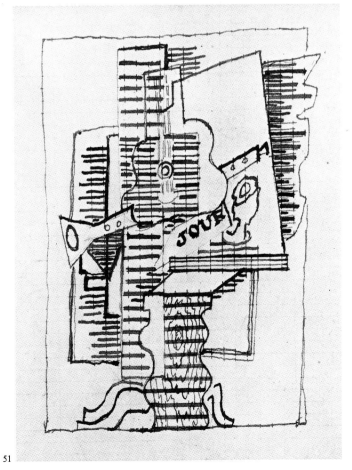

50   51

52. *The Musician*. 1917-18.
    Oil on canvas, 221.5×113 cm.
    Kunstmuseum, Basel.

53. *Guitar and Clarinet*. 1918.
    Paper and corrugated cardboard, 77×95 cm.
    Museum of Art, Philadelphia, Arensberg collection.

52

53

54

54. *Glass and Pear*. 1918.
    Oil on canvas, 46 × 33 cm.
    Perls Galleries, New York.

55. *Still Life with Grapes*. 1918.
    Oil on canvas, 49 × 65 cm.
    Private collection, U.S.A.

56. *Cubist Still Life (Guitar, Solo)*. 1919.
    Gouache on papier collé, 15 × 30 cm.
    Galerie Maeght, Paris.

57. *Musical Instruments and Fruit Dish*. 1919.
    Oil on canvas, 62 × 97 cm.
    Galeries Leiris, Paris.

55

56

57

58. *The Sideboard*. 1920.
   Oil on canvas, 81 × 100 cm.
   Galerie Beyeler, Basel.

59. *Woman*. 1920.
   Colored plaster, height 20 cm.
   Private collection.

60. *The Pedestal Table*. 1922.
   Oil on canvas, 192 × 71 cm.
   Metropolitan Museum of Art, New York.

61. *Fruit and Glass*. 1922.
   Oil on plywood, 26 × 65 cm.
   Private collection.

58

59

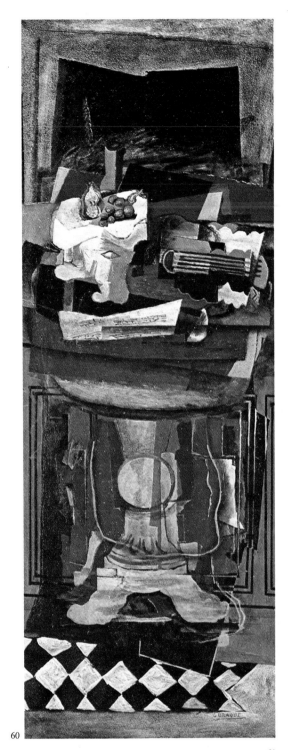

60

61

62-63. *The Canephorae*. 1922.
Oil on canvas, 180.5 × 73.5 cm.
Musée National d'Art Moderne, Paris.

64. *The Mantelpiece*. 1923.
Oil on canvas, 130 × 74 cm.
Kunsthaus, Zürich.

65. *Fruit, Jug, Pipe*. 1924.
Oil on canvas, 34 × 43 cm.
The Phillips Collection, Washington.

66. *The Basket of Flowers*. 1924.
Oil on canvas, 29.5 × 34.5 cm.
Private collection.

62

63

64

65

66

68

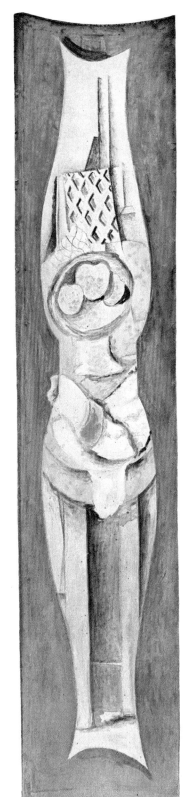

71

69 70

67. *The Marble Table*. 1925.
Oil on canvas, 130.5 × 75 cm.
Musée National d'Art Moderne, Paris.

68. *Fruit, Glass, Knife*. 1926.
Oil on canvas, 23 × 73 cm.
The Phillips Collection, Washington.

69. *Still Life with Fruit Dish*. 1926-27.
Oil on canvas, 192 × 43 cm.
Private collection.

70. *Still Life with Pitcher*. 1926-27.
Oil on canvas, 192 × 43 cm.
Private collection.

71. *Young Woman*. 1927.
Pastel on cloth-faced paper, 73 × 91 cm.
Private collection.

72

73

75

75. *Pedestal Table with Bottle of Rum*. 1930.
    Oil on canvas, 178 × 72 cm.
    Private collection.

76. *The Bathers*. 1931.
    Oil on plywood, 22 × 27 cm.
    Private collection.

77. *Recumbent Nude with Pedestal Table*. 1931.
    Oil on canvas, 24 × 41 cm.
    Private collection.

76

77

78. *Athena*. 1931.
   Oil on canvas, 39 × 33 cm.
   Private collection.

79. *Sao*. 1931.
   Incised plaster, 186 × 130 cm.
   Galerie Maeght, Paris.

80. *Heracles*. 1932.
   Incised plaster, 186 × 105 cm.
   Galerie Maeght, Paris.

81, 82 and 83. *Theogony (Vollard Suite)*. 1932.
   Etching, 36.8 × 29.7 cm.
   Galerie Maeght, Paris.

79

80

81

82

83

84

84. *The Pink Tablecloth*. 1933.
Oil and sand on canvas, 97 × 130 cm.
Chrysler Art Museum, Provincetown.

85. *Seated Woman*. 1934.
Etching, 24 × 18 cm.
Galerie Maeght, Paris.

85

86

87

86. *Still Life with Red Tablecloth*. 1934.
    Oil on canvas, 81 × 101 cm.
    Private collection.

87. *Woman with Easel*. 1936.
    Oil on canvas, 92 × 73 cm.
    Nathan Cummings Collection, Chicago.

88. *Woman with Mandolin*. 1937.
Oil on canvas, 130.2 × 97.2 cm.
Museum of Modern Art, New York.

89. *The Pedestal Table*. 1938.
Oil on canvas, 107 × 87 cm.
Private collection.

90. *The Boat with the Flag*. 1939.
Oil on canvas, 54 × 65 cm.
Private collection.

91. *Still Life with Palette*. 1939.
Oil on canvas, 72 × 89 cm.
Private collection.

92. *The Painter and His Model*. 1939.
Oil on canvas, 130 × 176 cm.
Private collection.

89

90

91

93. *The Two Mullets*. 1940-41.
    Oil on cloth-faced paper, 47×62 cm.
    Private collection.

94. *Carafe and Fish*. 1941.
    Oil on canvas, 33.5×55.5 cm.
    Musée National d'Art Moderne, Paris.

95. *Still Life with Skull*. 1941-45.
    Oil on canvas, 50×61 cm.
    Private collection.

93

94

95

96

96. *The Red Pedestal Table*. 1939-52.
Oil on canvas, 180×73 cm.
Musée National d'Art Moderne, Paris.

97. *Teapot and Grapes*. 1942.
Oil on canvas, 33×60.5 cm.
Galerie Maeght, Paris.

98. *Washstand in Front of the Window*. 1942.
Oil on canvas, 130×97 cm.
Musée National d'Art Moderne, Paris.

97

98

99

99. *Patience*. 1942.
    Oil on canvas, 145 × 113 cm.
    Goulandris Collection, Lausanne.

100. *The Man with the Guitar*. 1942-61.
     Oil on canvas, 130 × 97 cm.
     Private collection.

101. *Man with Easel*. 1942.
     Oil on cloth-faced paper, 100 × 81 cm.
     Quentin Laurens Collection.

102. *My Bike*. 1941-60.
     Oil on cloth-faced paper, 92 × 73 cm.
     Private collection.

103. *Still Life with Fish*. 1943.
     Oil on canvas, 29 × 48.5 cm.
     Galerie Maeght, Paris.

100

101

102

103

104

105

104. *Horse's Head*. 1941-42.
     Bronze, 42 × 91 × 17.5 cm.
     Musée National d'Art Moderne, Paris.

105. *The Ibis*. 1942-43.
     Bronze, height 18 cm.
     Musée National d'Art Moderne, Paris.

106. *Still Life with Ladder*. 1943.
     Oil on canvas, 92 × 73 cm.
     Private collection.

106

107

108

109

110

107. *The Billiard Table*. 1944.
 Oil and sand on canvas,
 130.5 × 195.5 cm.
 Musée National d'Art Moderne,
 Paris.

108. *The Drawing Room*. 1944.
 Oil on canvas, 120.5 × 150.5 cm.
 Musée National d'Art Moderne,
 Paris.

109. *The Billiard Table*. 1945.
 Oil on canvas, 116 × 89.5 cm.
 Private collection.

110. *The Billiard Table*. 1949.
 Oil on canvas, 145 × 195 cm.
 Museo de Arte Contemporáneo,
 Caracas.

111

111. *The Woman with a Book*. 1945.
Oil on canvas, 128 × 96 cm.
Private collection.

112. *The Plow*. 1945.
Oil on plywood, 22 × 27 cm.
Private collection.

113. *The Vase of Lilac*. 1946.
Oil on canvas, 81 × 54 cm.
Private collection.

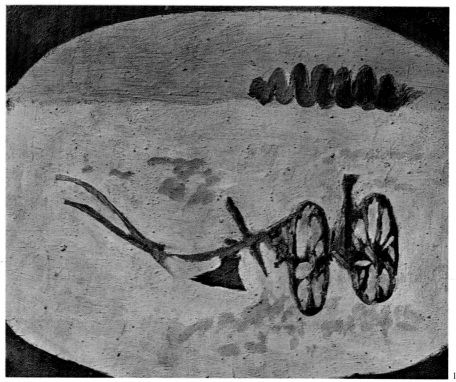

112

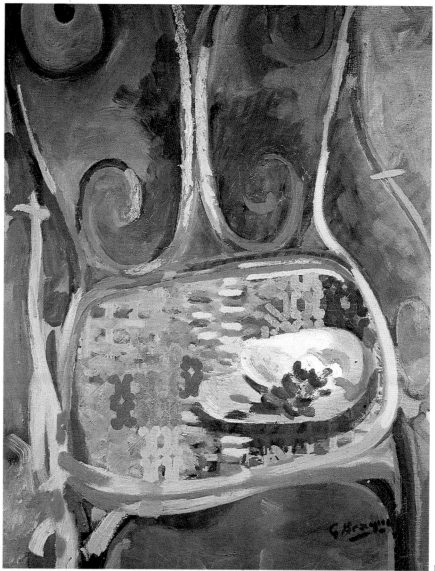

114

114. *The Mauve Garden Chair*. 1947-60.
Oil on canvas, 66 × 51 cm.
Private collection, New York.

115. *The Terrace*. 1948-61.
Oil on canvas, 97 × 130 cm.
Private collection.

116. *Still Life with Spiny Lobster*. 1948-50.
Oil on canvas, 162 × 73 cm.
Galerie Maeght, Paris.

115

117. *Studio I*. 1949.
   Oil on canvas, 92 × 73 cm.
   Private collection.

118. *Studio II*. 1949.
   Oil on canvas, 131 × 162.5 cm.
   Kunstsammlung Nordrhein-Westfalen, Düsseldorf.

119. *The Oysters*. 1949.
   Oil on canvas, 33 × 41 cm.
   Galerie Maeght, Paris.

117

118

119

120. *Studio IV*. 1949.
Oil on canvas, 130×195 cm.
Private collection, Basel.

121. *Reclining Woman*. 1930-52.
Oil on canvas, 74×180 cm.
Galerie Maeght, Paris.

120

121

123. *Studio III*. 1949-51.
 Oil on canvas, 145 × 175 cm.
 Private collection, Vaduz.

124. *Night*. 1951.
 Oil on canvas, 162.5 × 73 cm.
 Galerie Maeght, Paris.

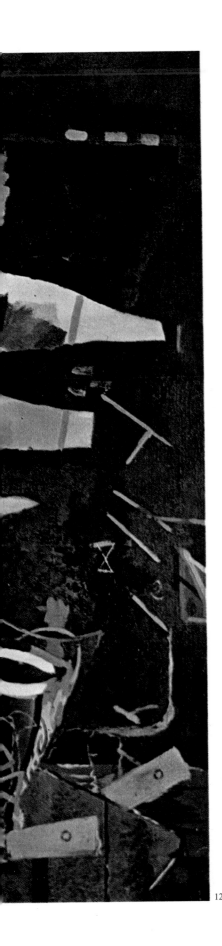

123

124

125

126

125. *The Aquarium*. 1951.
Oil on canvas, 100 × 81 cm.
Private collection.

126. *Fish*. 1944.
Bronze, length 34 cm.
Private collection.

127. *The Two Windows*. 1952.
Oil on canvas, 97 × 120.5 cm.
Perls Galleries, New York.

128. *Seashore, Varengeville*. 1952.
Oil on canvas, 25 × 65 cm.
Galerie Maeght, Paris.

127

128

129. *The Bird in Squares*. 1952-53.
Oil on canvas, 133 × 76 cm.
Private collection.

130. *The Blind*. 1954-61.
Oil on canvas, 162 × 72 cm.
Galerie Louise Leiris, Paris.

131. *Ajax*. 1954.
Oil on marouflé paper, 180 × 72 cm.
Private collection.

130

131

132

133

134

132. *The Echo*. 1953-56.
Oil on canvas, 130 × 162 cm.
Private collection.

133. *Palette and Flowers*. 1954-55.
Oil on canvas, 123.5 × 116 cm.
Museo de Arte Contemporáneo, Caracas.

134. *Study for the Ceiling of the Louvre*. 1953.
Oil on paper, 115 × 90 cm.
Galerie Maeght, Paris.

135. *The Plain*. 1955-56.
Oil on canvas, 20 × 73 cm.
Private collection.

136. *Landscape with Plow*. 1955.
Oil on canvas, 34 × 64 cm.
Galerie Maeght, Paris.

135

136

137. *Studio IX*. 1952-53-56.
   Oil on canvas, 146 × 146 cm.
   Musée National d'Art Moderne, Paris.

138. *The Black Birds*. 1956-57.
   Oil on canvas, 129 × 181 cm.
   Galerie Maeght, Paris.

139. *The Rape Field*. 1956-57.
   Oil on canvas, 20 × 65 cm.
   Private collection.

138

139

140

141

142

143

140. *The Fields (Low Sky)*. 1956-57.
Oil on canvas, 27 × 44.55 cm.
Private collection.

141. *Nest in the Foliage*. 1958.
Oil on canvas, 114 × 132 cm.
Galerie Maeght, Paris.

142. *Seashore*. 1958.
Oil on canvas, 31 × 65 cm.
Private collection.

143. *Landscape*. 1959.
Oil on canvas, 21 × 73 cm.
Galerie Maeght, Paris.

144

144. *The Birds in Flight*. 1959.
Oil on canvas, 72 × 162 cm.
Quentin Laurens Collection.

145, 146 and 147. *The Freedom of the Seas*. 1959.
Lithographs with text by P. Reverdy.
Galerie Maeght, Paris.

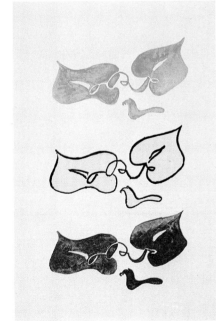

145

146

147

*le réveil,
la lumière
et la vie,
et plus que
tout la fin
de l'effroyable
rêve.*

Mirage

*Il ne pleut
plus que sur
les arbres
et sur ma
tête qui toute
est plus écla.*

148

148. *In Full Flight*. 1956-61.
   Oil on canvas, 114.5 × 170.5 cm.
   Musée National d'Art Moderne, Paris.

149. *The Birds*. 1960.
   Oil on canvas, 134 × 167.5 cm.
   Private collection.

150. *The Blue Aquarium*. 1960-62.
   Oil on canvas, 76 × 106 cm.
   Galerie Louise Leiris, Paris.

149

150

151

152

151. *Large Plow*. 1960.
Oil on canvas, 85 × 195 cm.
Galerie Maeght, Paris.

152. *The Boat*. 1960.
Oil on canvas, 38 × 78 cm.
Private collection.

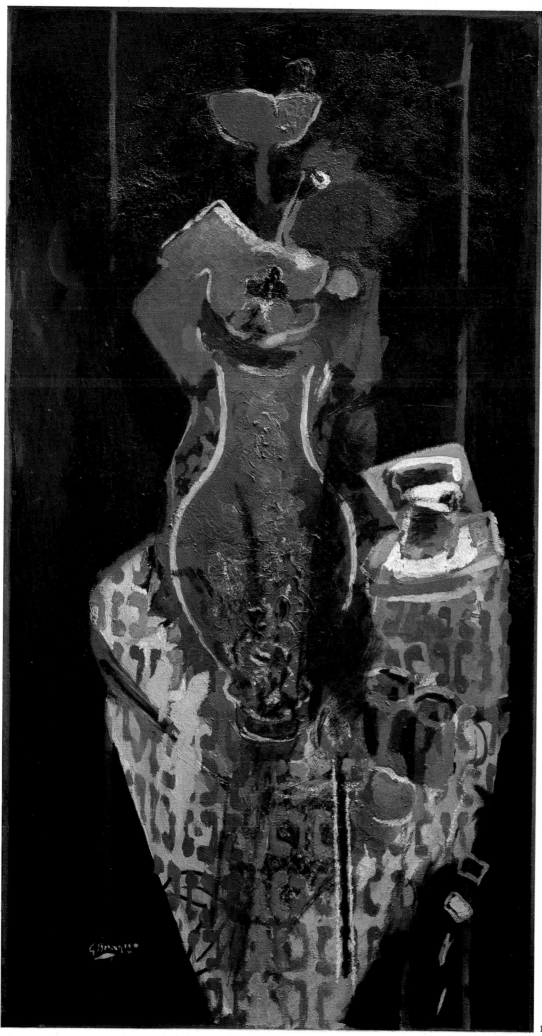

153

153. *Vase of Flowers on Red Tablecloth*. 1961.
Oil on canvas, 60.5 × 33 cm.
Galerie Maeght, Paris.

154. *The Plow*. 1961.
Oil on canvas, 19.5 × 33.5 cm.
Private collection.

155. *Bird in the Foliage*. 1961.
Lithograph, 80.5 × 105 cm.
Galerie Maeght, Paris.

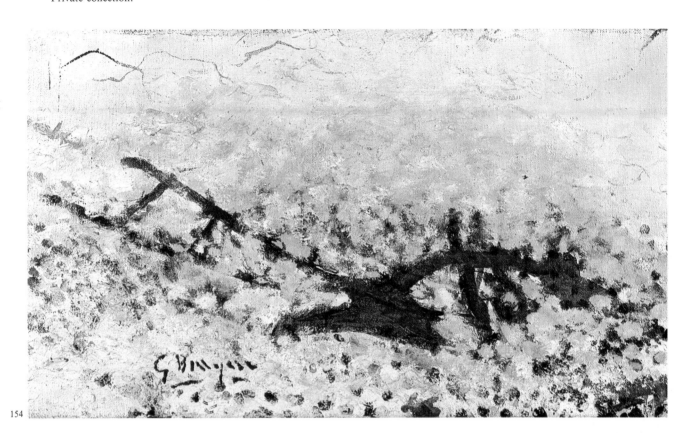

154

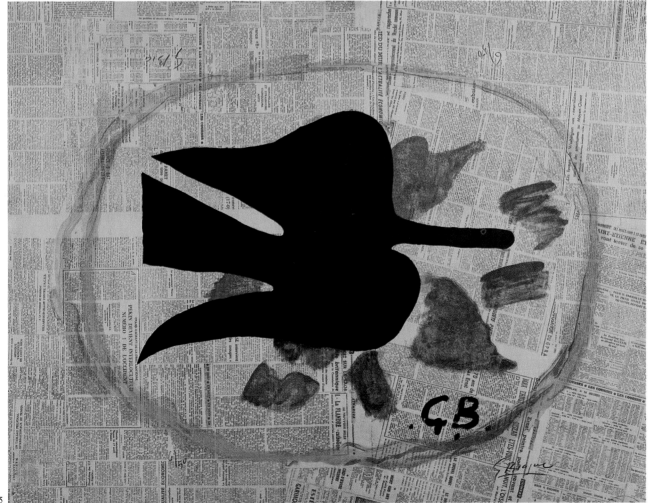

155

157

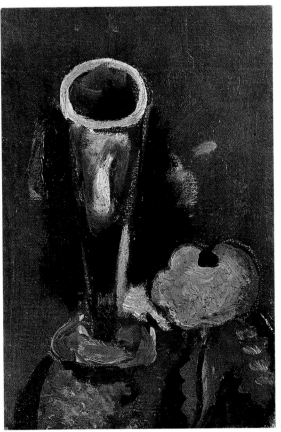

158

156. *The Bicycle*. 1961-62.
Oil on canvas, 147.5 × 99 cm.
Galerie Louise Leiris, Paris.

157. *The Turnwrest Plow*. 1962.
Oil on canvas, 33 × 40 cm.
Private collection.

158. *The Glass and the Apple*. 1962.
Oil on canvas, 24 × 16 cm.
Private collection.

LIST OF ILLUSTRATIONS

61. *Fruit and Glass*. 1922.
Oil on plywood, 26×65 cm.
Private collection.

62-63. *The Canephorae*. 1922.
Oil on canvas, 180.5×73.5 cm.
Musée National d'Art Moderne, Paris.

64. *The Mantelpiece*. 1923.
Oil on canvas, 130×74 cm.
Kunsthaus, Zürich.

65. *Fruit, Jug, Pipe*. 1924.
Oil on canvas, 34×43 cm.
The Phillips Collection, Washington.

66. *The Basket of Flowers*. 1924.
Oil on canvas, 29.5×34.5 cm.
Private collection.

67. *The Marble Table*. 1925.
Oil on canvas, 130.5×75 cm.
Musée National d'Art Moderne, Paris.

68. *Fruit, Glass, Knife*. 1926.
Oil on canvas, 23×73 cm.
The Phillips Collection, Washington.

69. *Still Life with Fruit Dish*. 1926-27.
Oil on canvas, 192×43 cm.
Private collection.

70. *Still Life with Pitcher*. 1926-27.
Oil on canvas, 192×43 cm.
Private collection.

71. *Young Woman*. 1927.
Pastel on cloth-faced paper, 73×91 cm.
Private collection.

72. *Still Life with Clarinet*. 1927.
Oil on canvas, 53×74 cm.
The Phillips Collection, Washington.

73. *The Three Boats*. 1929.
Oil on canvas, 24×35 cm.
Moderna Museet, Stockholm.

74. *The Pedestal Table*. 1929.
Oil on canvas, 146×113.5 cm.
The Phillips Collection, Washington.

75. *Pedestal Table with Bottle of Rum*.
1930.
Oil on canvas, 178×72 cm.
Private collection.

76. *The Bathers*. 1931.
Oil on plywood, 22×27 cm.
Private collection.

77. *Recumbent Nude with Pedestal Table*.
1931.
Oil on canvas, 24×41 cm.
Private collection.

78. *Athena*. 1931.
Oil on canvas, 39×33 cm.
Private collection.

79. *Sao*. 1931.
Incised plaster, 186×130 cm.
Galerie Maeght, Paris.

80. *Heracles*. 1932.
Incised plaster, 186×105 cm.
Galerie Maeght, Paris.

81, 82 and 83. *Theogony (Vollard Suite)*.
1932.
Etching, 36.8×29.7 cm.
Galerie Maeght, Paris.

84. *The Pink Tablecloth*. 1933.
Oil and sand on canvas, 97×130 cm.
Chrysler Art Museum, Provincetown.

85. *Seated Woman*. 1934.
Etching, 24×18 cm.
Galerie Maeght, Paris.

86. *Still Life with Red Tablecloth*. 1934.
Oil on canvas, 81×101 cm.
Private collection.

87. *Woman with Easel*. 1936.
Oil on canvas, 92×73 cm.
Nathan Cummings Collection, Chicago.

88. *Woman with Mandolin*. 1937.
Oil on canvas, 130.2×97.2 cm.
Museum of Modern Art, New York.

89. *The Pedestal Table*. 1938.
Oil on canvas, 107×87 cm.
Private collection.

90. *The Boat with the Flag*. 1939.
Oil on canvas, 54×65 cm.
Private collection.

91. *Still Life with Palette*. 1939.
Oil on canvas, 72×89 cm.
Private collection.

92. *The Painter and His Model*. 1939.
Oil on canvas, 130×176 cm.
Private collection.

93. *The Two Mullets*. 1940-41.
Oil on cloth-faced paper, 47×62 cm.
Private collection.

94. *Carafe and Fish*. 1941.
Oil on canvas, 33.5×55.5 cm.
Musée National d'Art Moderne, Paris.

95. *Still Life with Skull*. 1941-45.
Oil on canvas, 50×61 cm.
Private collection.

96. *The Red Pedestal Table*. 1939-52.
Oil on canvas, 180×73 cm.
Musée National d'Art Moderne, Paris.

97. *Teapot and Grapes*. 1942.
Oil on canvas, 33×60.5 cm.
Galerie Maeght, Paris.

98. *Washstand in Front of the Window*.
1942.
Oil on canvas, 130×97 cm.
Musée National d'Art Moderne, Paris.

99. *Patience*. 1942.
Oil on canvas, 145×113 cm.
Goulandris Collection, Lausanne.

100. *The Man with the Guitar*. 1942-61.
Oil on canvas, 130×97 cm.
Private collection.

101. *Man with Easel*. 1942.
Oil on cloth-faced paper, 100×81 cm.
Quentin Laurens Collection.

102. *My Bike*. 1941-60.
Oil on cloth-faced paper, 92×73 cm.
Private collection.

103. *Still Life with Fish*. 1943.
Oil on canvas, 29×48.5 cm.
Galerie Maeght, Paris.

104. *Horse's Head*. 1941-42.
Bronze, 42×91×17.5 cm.
Musée National d'Art Moderne, Paris.

105. *The Ibis*. 1942-43.
Bronze, height 18 cm.
Musée National d'Art Moderne, Paris.

106. *Still Life with Ladder*. 1943.
Oil on canvas, 92×73 cm.
Private collection.

107. *The Billiard Table*. 1944.
Oil and sand on canvas, 130.5×195.5 cm.
Musée National d'Art Moderne, Paris.

108. *The Drawing Room*. 1944.
Oil on canvas, 120.5×150.5 cm.
Musée National d'Art Moderne, Paris.

109. *The Billiard Table*. 1945.
Oil on canvas, 116×89.5 cm.
Private collection.

110. *The Billiard Table*. 1949.
Oil on canvas, 145×195 cm.
Museo de Arte Contemporáneo,
Caracas.

111. *The Woman with a Book*. 1945.
Oil on canvas, 128×96 cm.
Private collection.

112. *The Plow*. 1945.
Oil on plywood, 22×27 cm.
Private collection.

113. *The Vase of Lilac*. 1946.
Oil on canvas, 81×54 cm.
Private collection.

114. *The Mauve Garden Chair*. 1947-60.
Oil on canvas, 66×51 cm.
Private collection, New York.

115. *The Terrace*. 1948-61.
Oil on canvas, 97×130 cm.
Private collection.

116. *Still Life with Spiny Lobster*. 1948-50.
Oil on canvas, 162×73 cm.
Galerie Maeght, Paris.

117. *Studio I*. 1949.
Oil on canvas, 92×73 cm.
Private collection.

118. *Studio II*. 1949.
Oil on canvas, 131×162.5 cm.
Kunstsammlung Nordrhein-Westfalen,
Düsseldorf.

119. *The Oysters*. 1949.
Oil on canvas, 33×41 cm.
Galerie Maeght, Paris.

120. *Studio IV*. 1949.
Oil on canvas, 130×195 cm.
Private collection, Basel.

121. *Reclining Woman*. 1930-52.
Oil on canvas, 74×180 cm.
Galerie Maeght, Paris,

122. *Studio VI*. 1950-51
Oil on canvas, 130×162.5 cm.
Maeght Foundation, St-Paul-de-Vence.

123. *Studio III*. 1949-51.
Oil on canvas, 145×175 cm.
Private collection, Vaduz.

124. *Night*. 1951.
Oil on canvas, 162.5×73 cm.
Galerie Maeght, Paris.

125. *The Aquarium*. 1951.
Oil on canvas, 100×81 cm.
Private collection.

126. *Fish*. 1944.
Bronze, length 34 cm.
Private collection.

127. *The Two Windows*. 1952.
Oil on canvas, 97 × 120.5 cm.
Perls Galleries, New York.

128. *Seashore, Varengeville*. 1952.
Oil on canvas, 25 × 65 cm.
Galerie Maeght, Paris.

129. *The Bird in Squares*. 1952-53.
Oil on canvas, 133 × 76 cm.
Private collection.

130. *The Blind*. 1954-61.
Oil on canvas, 162 × 72 cm.
Galerie Louise Leiris, Paris.

131. *Ajax*. 1954.
Oil on marouflé paper, 180 × 72 cm.
Private collection.

132. *The Echo*. 1953-56.
Oil on canvas, 130 × 162 cm.
Private collection.

133. *Palette and Flowers*. 1954-55.
Oil on canvas, 123.5 × 116 cm.
Museo de Arte Contemporáneo,
Caracas.

134. *Study for the Ceiling of the Louvre*.
1953.
Oil on paper, 115 × 90 cm.
Galerie Maeght, Paris.

135. *The Plain*. 1955-56.
Oil on canvas, 20 × 73 cm.
Private collection.

136. *Landscape with Plow*. 1955.
Oil on canvas, 34 × 64 cm.
Galerie Maeght, Paris.

137. *Studio IX*. 1952-53-56.
Oil on canvas, 146 × 146 cm.
Musée National d'Art Moderne, Paris.

138. *The Black Birds*. 1956-57.
Oil on canvas, 129 × 181 cm.
Galerie Maeght, Paris.

139. *The Rape Field*. 1956-57.
Oil on canvas, 20 × 65 cm.
Private collection.

140. *The Fields (Low Sky)*. 1956-57.
Oil on canvas, 27 × 44.55 cm.
Private collection.

141. *Nest in the Foliage*. 1958.
Oil on canvas, 114 × 132 cm.
Galerie Maeght, Paris.

142. *Seashore*. 1958.
Oil on canvas, 31 × 65 cm.
Private collection.

143. *Landscape*. 1959.
Oil on canvas, 21 × 73 cm.
Galerie Maeght, Paris.

144. *The Birds in Flight*. 1959.
Oil on canvas, 72 × 162 cm.
Quentin Laurens Collection.

145, 146 and 147. *The Freedom of the Seas*.
1959.
Lithographs with text by P. Reverdy.
Galerie Maeght, Paris.

148. *In Full Flight*. 1956-61.
Oil on canvas, 114.5 × 170.5 cm.
Musée National d'Art Moderne, Paris.

149. *The Birds*. 1960.
Oil on canvas, 134 × 167.5 cm.
Private collection.

150. *The Blue Aquarium*. 1960-62.
Oil on canvas, 76 × 106 cm.
Galerie Louise Leiris, Paris.

151. *Large Plow*. 1960.
Oil on canvas, 85 × 195 cm.
Galerie Maeght, Paris.

152. *The Boat*. 1960.
Oil on canvas, 38 × 78 cm.
Private collection.

153. *Vase of Flowers on Red Tablecloth*.
1961.
Oil on canvas, 60.5 × 33 cm.
Galerie Maeght, Paris.

154. *The Plow*. 1961.
Oil on canvas, 19.5 × 33.5 cm.
Private collection.

155. *Bird in the Foliage*. 1961.
Lithograph, 80.5 × 105 cm.
Galerie Maeght, Paris.

156. *The Bicycle*. 1961-62.
Oil on canvas, 147.5 × 99 cm.
Galerie Louise Leiris, Paris.

157. *The Turnwrest Plow*. 1962.
Oil on canvas, 33 × 40 cm.
Private collection.

158. *The Glass and the Apple*. 1962.
Oil on canvas, 24 × 16 cm.
Private collection.